A LIFE IN BLOOM

A LIFE IN BLOOM

A Down-to-Earth Women's Guide to
a Successful Financial Future

Nancy Farran & Justin M. Dyer

ISBN: 1533610703
ISBN 13: 9781533610706

Disclaimer

This book is intended to provide accurate, informative, educational material about personal finance. Although the authors and the publisher have made every reasonable effort to ensure the accuracy of such information, individual situations vary, and readers should consult an appropriate professional with specific questions related to their personal finances and planning.

The authors, their employers, and the publisher assume no responsibility for errors, inaccuracies, omissions, or any inconsistency of specific applications to such individual situations, and disclaim any liability arising from the use or application of information contained in this book.

Neither the publisher nor the authors assume any responsibility for errors or for changes that may take place after publication.

The characters in these pages are fictional. Any resemblance to actual persons, living or dead, is coincidental, and any slights of people or organizations are unintended.

To the people who inspire me—my mother, my daughter, my sister, and those who trust me with their money and their stories. And to Justin, who keeps me balanced.
—*Nancy Farran*

To my wife Saleena, our children Zach and Zahra, and our entire family: Your love and support makes me want to be the best person I can be. And to Nancy, a truly remarkable woman and partner I am proud to call my friend.
—*Justin Dyer*

Table of Contents

About the Book

Another book on personal finance? Really?

We know, we know. The shelves are filled with personal finance books. Each one has its own angle. Why would we add to the groaning pile?

We work for a leading wealth management firm owned by one of North America's largest banks. Collectively we've racked up over fifty years of experience in the investment industry. Day after day, we see people make some great financial choices, but also many bad ones. We hear the same hopes and concerns:

- Will I have enough when I retire? What if I outlive my money?
- Will my family be okay? How can I help my kids financially?
- What are the basics of investing? What are the risks?
- How much can I spend? How much should I save?
- Can I be responsible with money but still have fun?

Our clients often ask us to recommend a good book on the basics of investing and financial planning. They want to know more, but they don't want to take a long course and they certainly don't want to read a textbook.

We explain certain concepts over and over; we dole out advice here, tips there. Finally, it occurred to us. Why not pull it all together? Why not put our words to paper? Then we'll have that good book our clients are looking for.

Our goal is to give you practical information, from a Canadian vantage point, about personal finance. Think of this information as the ground, solid and reliable. Over it, we spread the topsoil of our opinions, enriched by years of observing real-life people and real-world results. The result: a garden plot in which you can plant your financial future.

What makes this book different?

All books on personal finance are educational. But let's be honest—some are a chore to read. We're passionate about our subject, and we wanted that passion—that spark—to fire up our book and lift it above the ordinary. Naturally we want you to learn, but we also want you to think. What kind of person are you? What matters to you? *Who* matters to you? And we want you to dream: What will your future look like? Your family's future? What kind of legacy will you leave?

So what gives our book that spark?

- *Conversational language.* Every day, clients meet with us to talk about their finances. To *talk*. In this book, we have a conversation with you about your financial future. We ask you lots of questions. We share our thoughts and experiences. We use ordinary language and try to steer clear of the jargon our industry is famous for.
- *A story.* Our brains respond powerfully to stories. We pay attention to them and we remember them. Woven through our book is a fictional story that echoes our metaphor of finance, gardening, responsibility, dreams, and passion. We hope it keeps you turning the pages, and we especially hope it illustrates the deep connection between financial responsibility and a rich, blooming life.

Why focus on women?

Years ago a female client told Justin something that has stuck with him ever since. She was a widow and had been on her own for two years. "You're the man in my life now," she said. "You have to look after my money for me." Her words not only touched Justin, they reminded him why he is dedicated to helping people, especially women, with their finances.

Anyone can read, learn from, and enjoy this book. However, time and experience have shown us that women need to be part of the financial discussion in a different way.

Women live longer than men. They're increasingly in charge of their own finances, and often those of their aging parents. Many lead busy lives, juggling big jobs and many demands. We want women to learn how to discover and follow the right financial track and to do all they can to make their futures secure.

Many of our clients are women who are single, divorced, or widowed. They're making financial decisions on their own. Some never had to deal with the money side of life before, but now they do and they need help. That's where we come in.

As a woman recently said to Nancy, "I listen politely to friends and family, but it's your advice that I take to heart and act on. I can't thank you enough."

About the Authors

Nancy Farran

My Scottish father taught me a lot about money, and a lot about life. Consider my embarrassment when my Grade 2 teacher asked every student to recite a well-known proverb and explain its meaning. I patiently awaited my turn while the other kids took theirs: "Too many cooks spoil the broth." "A stitch in time saves nine." On and on it went. When at last I stood before the class, I proudly declared, "Mony a mickle maks a muckle." A sea of blank faces stared at me. No one had the faintest idea what I'd said.

How could my classmates not know this Scottish adage? It was simple: Lots of little bits add up to one big bit—a muckle. (Or, as Dad often muttered in his strong brogue, "To hell with poverty!")

I owe my father a debt of gratitude. He bought me my first mining stock when I was eight. From then on, while other kids read the funny papers, I read the financial pages. Were it not for his inspiration, and the common sense he instilled in me so early, I would not have become a financial advisor and vice-president of a major investment house today.

Writing this book reminded me of the lesson I learned in Grade 2: When you talk about money, use words and ideas that everyone understands. In this book, we use simple language (and no Scottish brogue) to explore how families shape our money beliefs, how we all hold different values around money, and how our beliefs and values can keep our finances on track—or derail them.

Justin Dyer

They say the apple doesn't fall far from the tree. My father was a compliance officer for a large stock brokerage firm, and my mother was an assistant to two successful stock brokers. Not surprisingly, I've always been interested in money. As a child, I wanted to have it and spend it, but I soon became fascinated with how to make it grow.

When I was ten, my mom and I entered the local newspaper's stock market challenge. Each participant chose four stocks, one from each market sector. The game lasted three months, and it was the most exciting thing I'd ever done. I quickly got into the habit of pulling out the newspaper's financial section to check my stocks (my ritual to this day). By the time the challenge ended, I'd learned a lot.

By age eleven, I was reading investment books and market gurus' newsletters. I was probably the only fifth-grader who knew what a put or call option was. It's fair to say I had a pretty good grasp of how the market worked.

After school, I'd sometimes visit my mom downtown at the office. The huge room, called the pit, was crammed with desks and pink and blue pieces of paper and people yelling and taking telephone orders before handing them off to a runner en route to the trading desk. When I was eighteen, my father arranged for me to visit the commodity trading floor to see the action first-hand. Again, it was mayhem. I loved it.

I considered buying myself a seat on the trading floor but decided to finish my education instead. As a financial advisor and planner, I play a different role than the stock brokers and commodity traders I watched as a child, but it's every bit as exciting.

Part One: Preparing

In the Garden

Rose knelt on a thick foam pad, but her knees were talking to her anyway. Her back too.

You're fifty-three, Mom. What do you expect? Laurel's voice was also talking to her, as it often did when her daughter wasn't around. From her very first word, Laurel had always been a talker, and she dispensed advice the way some politicians scatter promises—that is to say, freely, whether invited or not. But it was a good thing. Her daughter's lecturing over the past year had pulled Rose through the Great Unmooring, as she thought of it. With capital letters.

Rose's hands grew black with soil as she trowelled out the dried-up lobelia. She hated gardening gloves, preferred the honest feel of loose earth any day. The foam kneeling pad, she accepted. So too the polo shirts emblazoned with the garden centre's logo, a stylized open tulip. And the khaki pants that complete the dull staff uniform, and the decidedly unfeminine steel-toed safety shoes she had to wear. But no way was she going to spend her days sweating inside tight gloves, her fingers swelling up like boiled bratwurst.

With a twist, she rooted out the last few brown blossoms. Who in their right mind put this planter in the full-sun display anyhow?

It was one more mistake, one more bad decision at the garden centre that she was so excited to join three months ago. Then it had looked like the perfect job: shrubs and flowers, seeds and seedlings, all day, every day. Pruning and watering, planting mixed baskets, advising customers. All things she loved to do. And she got paid for it.

Now, though, she saw things she'd never noticed back when she was just another customer dropping in on the way home for an assortment of bulbs or a flat of annuals. She saw the mixed-up seed displays; the dry, forgotten shrubs in the corner; the prices on the floor that didn't match the ones in the computer. She saw customers leave because they couldn't find anyone to help them. She saw Jake, the after-school part-timer with the ear buds surgically attached, who arrived late and left early every single day.

Rose was a lot of things she'd rather not be: middle-aged, a size bigger than last year, mechanically hopeless, and of course, now, single. But there was no denying she was organized. To a fault, Laurel would say, though she was one to talk. Laurel had meticulousness in her genes, and she could thank those genes for her career as an accountant.

Rose was organized, and the Blooming Tulip Garden Centre was not. And the inefficiency was slowly driving her insane.

"There you are!" This voice was real, not inside Rose's head. Jasmine glided into view, too-big polo shirt floating out from her waif-like frame, and put her hands on her hips. "Your cell phone's turned off again."

Rose set down her trowel and smiled. "Don't lecture me, young lady."

"Honestly. Laurel's been trying to get you all morning. She finally called me instead. Can you babysit the twins tonight or should she book me?"

"I can do it." Rose considered. "Unless you need the money."

Jasmine shook her head, her tiny beaded braids swinging. "Nuh-uh. I've got more important stuff. Yoga after work, then I'm meeting Sadie at the new juice bar. You try it yet?"

Rose coughed to cover the sound of gagging. She loved grass and herbs more than most people did, but why anyone would want to swill them down in vile-tasting liquid form was beyond her.

"Look, I gotta run. I'm on cash." Jasmine took two steps, then turned back. "Oh hey, there's news. We got a buyer."

Rose's eyebrows knit together. "What do you mean?"

"The garden centre. It's been bought. Someone named Mrs. Birch. Hysterical, huh? A Mrs. Birch running a garden centre?"

Bought? Since when was the centre even up for sale? It was the first Rose had heard about it.

"Oh, and she's here." Jasmine waved her hand toward the main sales area. "Up front. She's got some guy with her. Older, maybe your age, but like, kind of studly. You should check it out."

—❦—

GARDENERS

Are you wondering how a fictional character named Rose figures in a book about personal finance? As you'll see, Rose and the other characters in these pages face many of the same questions about financial security, planning, and a rewarding life as do you, your family, and your friends.

It's no coincidence that many characters in this book are gardeners. Personal finance and gardening have a lot in common. If you choose and nurture them well, the seeds you plant now can bear flowers and fruit for a lifetime. In the same way, the seed money you invest today can produce big dividends later. Nature reminds us to be patient and to trust. Global markets do the same. Gardeners are patient optimists, burying bulbs deep in the dirt, watching tiny shoots push past obstacles with toughness and resilience. Investors, too, know that despite occasional bumps, markets historically trend upwards.

We hope that the advice in this book, and the fictional story that winds through it, will help you grow the garden of your life. We want you to recognize any weed-choked, stony ground that may be holding you back from financial freedom. We want to give you the tools to till, fertilize, and plant your financial garden, then nurture and protect it until it produces gorgeous blossoms.

⊷⊶

DREAMS

Dreams are important. They allow us to visualize what and where we'd like to be at some point in the future. Making your dreams come true involves taking a number of small but bold steps. We'll come to those later. For now, let yourself dream for a few moments and see where your dreams take you.

How would your life change if you were wealthy? What would affluence feel like? How would you lavish your largesse? Would you keep the same job? Buy a larger house, or one with a view? Travel the world? Pay for someone's education? Drink better wine?

Before you can answer those questions, you need to define what wealth means to you. For you, how much—or how little—it would take?

How do you get that money? Many of us dream about one day holding the winning lotto ticket. We assume a windfall will set us up for life, but that's not necessarily the case. Some studies show that a few years after winning the lottery, up to 70% of winners are broke. Other studies show that money we earn through our own efforts is money we tend to keep, much more so than funds that land in our laps.

Rarely are dreams suddenly answered. To turn dreams into reality, you need specific, realistic, attainable goals and a plan to reach them. Otherwise, dreams usually stay just that—dreams.

We want you to achieve and live your dreams. We also want you to gain enough confidence and knowledge to improve your financial life and the lives of those you care about. That's why we wrote this book.

—⸗—

WOMEN

We wrote this book with women in mind, and the main fictional characters are women. In our financial management business, we work with a lot of women. In our experience, they are typically the ones seeking out the kind of financial advice this book provides.

That said, the information we've gathered here can benefit everyone: women and men of any age. We encourage you to share this book and what you learn with anyone who cares about a secure future. Many don't know how much of a nest egg they need for retirement, let alone have a plan for accumulating it.

Whether you're a woman or a man, the only sure way to become financially secure is to learn about money, make smart choices, and rely on yourself. That's a cold, hard fact.

We hear the chorus of female voices: "But I don't earn as much as a man." Sadly, that's true. Women often make less money than their male counterparts, as much as one-fifth less according to some studies. Fortunately, it's not what you earn but what you *save* that matters most in attaining wealth. Our earlier message is worth repeating: The seeds you plant today can bear flowers and fruit for a lifetime.

———

A LIFE IN BLOOM

We're not trying to sell ourselves or any get-rich-quick scheme with this book. Our aim is simple: We want to demystify money for women, to talk about financial planning in simple language, and to use examples and terms that resonate with women and apply worldwide. We're passionate about improving your financial literacy, no matter who you are or where you're starting from.

We believe that the optimism and confidence you gain from reading these pages will help you plant and nurture your financial garden, and reap a bountiful harvest. We believe that you, like others we've worked with, can enjoy a life in bloom—a life rich in happiness, in satisfaction, and in wealth.

2

Who You Are

"I'm Mrs. Birch."

The long-legged woman with the mane of silver-white hair extended her hand. Rose saw short but beautifully manicured nails and an elegant silver band that looked like a leaf circling the woman's middle finger. "Pleased to meet you—" the woman peered at Rose's name tag—"Rose."

The new owner of the Blooming Tulip was imposing, to say the least. Nearly six feet tall, by Rose's guess, and not trying to hide it. High cheekbones, loose limbs, a creamy complexion etched with faint lines that showed her age yet somehow added to her beauty. She must be, what? Late sixties, early seventies? When Jasmine said they had a buyer, Rose had pictured some business-suited young tycoon. Instead, everything about this smartly dressed woman, from her posture to her silver earrings and tall calfskin boots, telegraphed age, poise, and elegance.

"Welcome aboard. We—we're happy you're here," said Rose.

Sheesh. How lame was that? She was terrible, downright hopeless, at small talk. Sure, the right words came, but always hours later, when she lay awake in bed reliving the day's failed conversations. Laurel was the talker in their family, not her. Frank used to remind Rose of that every chance he could.

But Mrs. Birch was paying little attention to Rose or any of the half-dozen employees gathered around. She was sizing up the place, a regal queen surveying her kingdom. Rose tried to see the garden centre through the new owner's eyes: the jumble of unshelved houseplants to one side of the entrance, the abandoned carts and dolleys blocking the aisles, the wet, dirt-smeared counter in front of the single open cash.

Mrs. Birch brought her gaze back to the group. "Looks like we've got our work cut out for us."

Rose could feel her co-workers stiffen. Except for the part-time slacker kids, who wouldn't arrive until fifteen minutes into their shift, they were a good bunch—reliable, loyal, hard workers. Every one of them knew why the Blooming Tulip was in shambles, and it wasn't because of them.

Mrs. Birch, as if sensing their defensiveness, cocked her head. "I'm guessing there's not one of you here who's afraid of work." Then she smiled.

It was like the sun blazing forth after an endless grey stretch of rain. When Mrs. Birch smiled, she went from elegant to dazzling, and somehow Rose knew things would never be the same again.

⚬⚬

MONEY ATTITUDES

When it comes to money, what sort of person are you? Do you learn from your mistakes? Do you have a rainy-day fund? Do you spend impulsively on whatever catches your eye? Do you have trouble deciding what to do with your money?

Think back to your childhood. How did your parents handle money? Their fears may have become your fears. Their joys may have become your joys. As the twig is bent, so grows the tree, whether you routinely put money aside or live from paycheque to paycheque.

When you were young, did you get a weekly allowance, receive gifts of money for your birthday, earn a little cash from babysitting or odd jobs? What did you do with that money? Did you save a little, spend a little? You may not realize it, but your attitude toward money was shaped by the first quarters and dollars you called your own.

Some parents train their children to divide up their money, 10% for charity, 10% for long-term savings, and some for spending now. While that's commendable, it's a textbook approach that doesn't always work in real life. If you were raised with that sort of advice, it may have turned you into the great money manager you are today—or the reckless one.

Understanding who you are when it comes to money requires a journey of self-exploration. This chapter takes you on that trip. First we'll explore the most common money fears that people have. Then we'll describe the different investment personalities we've met in our work.

Which fears are your fears? Which personality type are you? The answers to those questions will give you some of the key tools you need to plan and tend your financial garden.

TOP TEN FEARS

Who doesn't want more money and fewer financial worries? Yet defeatist attitudes keep many people from achieving their personal best. *I've always been poor and always will be. There's no use trying to better myself. I know I'll*

never succeed. I'm not like people who have money. I don't deserve it. Or, I've al-
ways overspent my income. I'll never curb my impulsive buying.

The continuous loop of negative thoughts may be subconscious, but it's very real. It keeps people from what they deserve: the greatest possible degree of happiness.

Many people share the same fears about money. Often these fears are deep-rooted, propelling you forward or holding you back. If your fears impact your life in a major way, they may need professional attention.

1. Fear of having too little

Many people are afraid of not having enough. Before you can define *enough*, you have to determine what you need and what you already have. Until then, you'll feel nervous about your financial future.

The fear of having too little is often tied to fears of being rootless, homeless, or dependent on others. Even wealthy, established individuals can harbour secret fears of being homeless and penniless, toting their few possessions around in shopping bags. This fear is closely related to the valid concern financial advisors often hear: clients are afraid they'll outlast their money.

2. Fear of having too much

Maybe you're afraid to succeed financially. Maybe you choose not to attract wealth, and do so in subtle and not-so-subtle ways. You may worry that money will change you and you'll lose your friends, or that your friends won't know you or will want something from you. You may worry that success will draw attention to you or make you a target for thieves.

Silly? If you fear having too much, this won't sound silly to you.

3. Fear of having to make decisions

Do you find it easier to go with the flow? Does being the one to paddle the canoe feel like . . . work? Do you usually think that things will sort themselves out? Or that someone else can make the decisions, maybe someone you live with?

Stand outside yourself and try to see patterns that may have been with you since childhood. Perhaps you weren't allowed to make decisions because you might make a mistake. For many people, the fear of making decisions is linked to the fear of failure. We all make mistakes; how we deal with them is what matters. Maybe you have trouble forgiving yourself, learning from your errors, and moving forward.

4. Fear of delegating

Unless you're a financial expert, there are likely gaps in what you know about money. Do you fear those gaps or feel ashamed of them? Do you know you need help planning your future prosperity but are afraid to admit it? What if an expert you work with discovers that you don't know everything, or even much, about money? What will that person think of you if you delegate every financial decision?

It can be hard to trust others, particularly when your money's at stake. But most people need financial advice at some point, whether from a book, trusted friends or family, or certified professionals.

5. Fear of being vulnerable

This deep-rooted fear is similar to the fear of delegating, because it's all about trust. Feeling vulnerable can be difficult. It can be uncomfortable to show the world your soft underbelly or confess to a lack of knowledge. Underneath, you may fear that someone will take advantage of you, and that's a scary idea.

Some people react to this fear by blindly trusting and hoping for the best. Others assume a fetal position and do nothing. How do you deal with this fear?

6. Fear of feeling poor

Do you sometimes spend money to make others, and even yourself, believe that you have more? Do you always pick up the cheque at lunch, or leave overly generous tips? Do you take taxis rather than buses, buy far too many shoes, support a daily latte habit? Any one of these little extravagances can make you feel sinfully rich. They're like reassurances that you'll never know poverty.

The trouble is, you may be so afraid of feeling poor that you spend more than you should, including money you don't have. Being afraid of feeling poor can lead to *being* poor. As investment guru Warren Buffett once said, "Only when the tide goes out do you discover who's been swimming naked."

7. Fear of deserving

Why do some people earn $10 an hour while others earn $400? Why were you born into a family that left you money while your best friend never has a dime? Why were you lucky enough to have parents who scrimped so that you could go to the best schools?

The world is an uneven place. Some get more than others, as unfair as it may seem. Maybe you attribute your success to having been lucky, having had breaks, having benefited from good timing. Maybe you believe you've deceived others into thinking you're competent. How does that make you feel? Can you accept your good fortune with grace? Should you try to give back? If so, how much should you give? As with any other phobia, the fear of deserving can be emotionally crippling.

8. Fear of living too long

Some people are afraid they will live so long that they'll end up alone and unloved in a care facility no one can find. If only your life had a "best before" or "use by" date, you might breathe a little easier. The truth is, you can't predict the last days or years of your life.

The fear of living too long can make you too conservative in your investment choices. *What if I lose money?* you may worry. *I can't afford to lose money.* If you're afraid of outliving your money, you may severely curtail your life: *I can't take an exotic vacation. I can't buy a new car. I can't go to the movies. I can't, I can't, I can't.*

9. Fear of dying young

This is the opposite of the previous fear. Feeling sure that you'll die young can create a fatalism that's heartbreaking to watch. This fear may give you a "do it now" or "live for the moment" attitude in which you see saving and planning as a waste of time. You bury your fears under another glass of wine, spending and partying today because you could be gone tomorrow.

If you watched your parents or grandparents die prematurely, you know what this fear can do to your psyche.

10. Fear of numbers

Are you afraid of numbers? Do logic, probability, and mathematical progressions make you feel dizzy and out of your depth?

Innumeracy, or mathematical illiteracy, can have serious consequences for you and other smart people. It can paralyze you and keep you from making wise, numbers-based decisions. Math phobia and an overall lack of confidence when it comes to numbers can make a strong person weak, and an easy target for con artists to exploit.

———— ✿ ————

Which of these ten fears grips you? One of them? Several?

The best gardens are planned out, and the best gardeners know something about the plants they work with. The good news is that early, sound financial planning, and learning more about the world of money, can lessen or resolve all of the top ten money fears.

As this book goes on, we'll explore what you can do to overcome your fears about money.

FOUR INVESTMENT PERSONALITIES

Ever since Freud observed and recorded patterns in human behaviour, psychologists have pegged individuals by personality type. It's no surprise that your attitudes and decisions about money, rational and irrational alike, reflect your investment personality.

Behavioural economists study how who you are affects what you do when it comes to spending, disbursing, saving, and investing money. They also examine how individuals' economic decisions can affect global market returns.

Here's an example. The time-tested advice, based on historical patterns, is to buy when the market is down and sell when the market is up. Yet hordes of people ignore that advice. They feel more secure when they're feverishly scrambling to buy the same rising stock everyone else is buying. The higher prices go, the more people want to join in the feeding frenzy. That, as Mr. Spock might say, is illogical. But when emotion overrides logic, look out.

Emotion and money are often a poor fit. You may know this, yet you may still respond the way your psychic makeup and experience have conditioned you to respond.

Over our many years of advising clients and friends about financial decisions, we've noticed four distinct investment personalities. Which one are you?

1. Paralysis by Analysis personality

We're big fans of research. But we're also big fans of getting things done. The Paralysis by Analysis investment personality needs lots of information and lots of time before making a decision. This is the most difficult personality type that we see.

Some decisions in life need to be made on a timely basis. When market conditions demand a quick response, many advisors first call clients who act decisively and well, then call clients who may or may not act on sound advice. If you never act on advice, your phone may not ring as often. Your inability to decide may work against you.

Here's what we recommend if you're this personality type: Set a realistic deadline and promise yourself, or others, that you'll make a decision by that time on that date. As you get closer, be prepared for a little anxiety, or even a lot. Trust yourself. Make a decision and move on. Then make another decision. Before you know it, the process should get easier.

We'll add an important caveat. If you need to make a decision and others are pressing you to act, make sure they have your best interests at heart. Whatever the issue, use your good judgment in knowing whom to trust, whether with your heart, your children, your wallet, or your retirement. Once you've done that, decision making will be much easier. Sometimes the right thing to do is nothing. But not always.

2. Spontaneous personality

Say you visit the hairstylist for a trim, but after glancing at magazines you emerge as a redhead. Or you see a piece about whales in the news and immediately decide to devote your life to saving the whales. Or you buy a pair of eye-catching lined boots in July on the assumption that this winter (or next) could be extra-cold.

Sound familiar? Then you likely have a Spontaneous investment personality. This personality type has few fears in the moment but may suffer paralyzing fears in the dark of night. Does money keep you awake?

Spontaneity can be fun, but be careful. Impetuous investment choices often spell trouble. You may insist on pursuing a tip you heard at a cocktail party, thus undoing a carefully thought-out investment strategy. Passion is admirable, but unbridled passion can wreck a solid financial plan or investment portfolio.

If you're the spontaneous type, recognize your nature. Allow some budget room for the needs that weren't there yesterday but are compelling today. Ask the shoe store to hold those boots for a couple of hours; then call a friend for a second opinion. As for that great investment idea, before you proceed, clarify your thoughts. Jot down five compelling reasons to pursue the idea. Do your reasons make good sense?

Even if you're breaking new ground, a trustworthy financial advisor will want to make sure you maintain a steady path. Your path, as a Spontaneous personality, may be less straight than others', but you will get there.

3. Greed-is-Good personality
Just as we're big fans of research and getting things done, we're also big fans of drive, desire, achievement, and other worthy pursuits. Greed has a place in that spectrum, but not if it's your sole motivator.

The "me first" Greed-is-Good investment personality is often unattractive. We know very few people motivated by greed alone, and very few people who want to be. Greed can cause irrational behaviour and pain. It can also result in poor portfolio performance. Maybe you know someone who believed in the huge returns promised by a get-rich-quick scheme, but then the scheme—and its dreams—turned to dust.

Our advice if you're this personality type? Exercise caution. The road to getting rich quick is often paved with bad intentions. We don't believe in "get rich quick." We believe in "get rich in an orderly fashion."

4. Balanced personality

The person who takes a balanced approach to investment is the person financial advisors all want to see.

If you're a Balanced investment personality, you always do your homework. At the very least, you research the people you're considering to manage your money.

You ask thoughtful questions, and you may seek a second opinion before committing to a plan. But you're decisive. You recognize that not every decision you make will be perfect, but if most of your big decisions are sound, all will be well.

You recognize that markets go up and down, and while you prefer the ups, you don't panic at the downs. You're rational and don't fear change. Knowing you're in this for the long haul, you avoid the short-term buzz. You're patient and prepared to wait as you watch your money grow.

A little caution is natural. Even the wealthiest people can be nervous about global markets and institutions sometimes. Building self-confidence—*realistic* self-confidence—will help you become a Balanced investment personality.

As Mrs. Birch outlined her plans—they'd close for a week to get the place in shape, then reopen with a giant sale that would draw people into the revamped store—the staff began to relax.

"It won't be easy, and it won't be quick." Mrs. Birch scanned the faces of her new staff. "This place has been mismanaged for years. It'll take more than spit and polish and a big sale to put us in the black. But it's going to happen. I've turned around a lot of businesses, and I've got a good feeling about this one. But I need every one of you to pull your weight. Are you with me?"

Rose nodded and let out her breath. Looking around, she realized she wasn't the only one who'd been worried about layoffs.

"That's a relief," Jasmine whispered. "I need this job."

Rose needed it too. Once again the familiar doubts kicked in: should she have held out for alimony after Frank left last year? She'd been so angry, so hurt and stunned at his announcement out of nowhere, over eggs one morning, that it was finished, thirty-three years together gone in a swipe, like grime off a mirror, that she just wanted out, to sever all ties and move on. She couldn't stand the idea of getting paycheques from Frank—being paid to stay away, it felt like—so she'd accepted a lump sum, sunk most of it into a small, rundown condo, invested the rest with help from Laurel, and landed a full-time job at the Blooming Tulip. From now on, she would earn her own way.

"There you are, Lawrence. Finally." Mrs. Birch turned toward the lanky man who had just come through the sliding doors. Her voice was rimmed with frost. "I was going to tell everyone about the landscape design division you're heading up, but why don't you do it yourself."

The attractive man strode toward them. Isolated details hit her first: the deeply tanned skin, the cropped brown hair tipped with silver, the long-sleeved T-shirt that fit close enough to confirm that yes, he worked hard, eyes like the bluest mountain lake. Rose took him in, and her stomach fell like a broken elevator.

It must have shown, because he approached her first. Held out his hand. "Tripp," he said. He looked straight at her, unblinking.

Her insides plunged another few floors. *Trip?* What was that supposed to mean? Her mind raced. As she puzzled over the word, she grasped his hand, strong and mitten-warm.

"Not Lawrence." He continued to stare. "I go by Tripp."

3

Good Gardeners

How many times had she hit "Mom" on her smart phone only to get no answer? Four? Five? A hundred?

With one eye on the nineteen emails that had come in since her 8 AM meeting—how could there be so many when practically everyone had been in the boardroom with her all morning?—Laurel checked her phone. No missed calls.

She'd try one more time, then break down and pay Jasmine to watch the boys tonight. It would mean no takeout coffee for a week, since she'd already used up this month's babysitting budget, but so be it. Tonight was important. And Jasmine was willing. She'd said so when she took Laurel's message at the garden centre.

That was half an hour ago, and Mom still hadn't called back and she wasn't answering now. Laurel squirmed with impatience. What's the point of having a cell phone if you never turn it on? She had asked her mother that many times, but Rose would just smile and shrug. "*I like being out of touch sometimes,*" she'd say.

That's how it was with her mother. Yes, she was loving and supportive, always. Laurel only made it through that long, lost year after Matthew died because her mother took the twins, just babies then, while Laurel clawed her way up from the frightening pit of widowhood. But honestly. When Laurel showed her mother how to pay bills online, or explained compound interest for the third time, or hunted around for better car insurance because Rose didn't want to upset the nice young agent who'd sold her a ridiculously expensive package, Laurel felt as if she were the parent and her mom was the child.

Well, Laurel had children of her own, twin boys who at seven and a half generated the noise and mess of four kids, and they needed a sitter. She called the garden centre again, resigned to booking Jasmine and enduring burnt coffee in the staff kitchen for a week.

"Blooming Tulip. Can I help you?"

"Mom? Is that you?"

"Honey! I'm sorry, I was going to call you back. It's just—well, there's a lot going on here. Jasmine said you need me to stay with the boys."

"Could you? I won't be out late." Laurel cleared her throat. "Well, I mean I could be. Probably not. But maybe. It depends."

"Oh, I get it. You have a date. One of those World Wide Web things?"

Laurel sighed. "It's called the Internet, Mom. Internet dating. Please. You can't possibly be that out of touch."

Rose chuckled. "I can come around four, four-thirty."

"Make it five. The boys have soccer, and I missed the gym yesterday so I've got to fit in a workout while they're on the field. And we need groceries." Five more emails sailed in, three of them with attachments. "And I have to catch up on email. Okay, gotta dash. There's a latte with my name on it."

———✸———

When it comes to others' financial affairs, you can't always believe what you see. People who are wealthy may be humble and unassuming. People whose finances are a muddle may pretend to have more than they do.

So how can you recognize the smart investors out there? What traits make them good at planting and nurturing their financial gardens? More important, what can you learn from them? Can you develop the same traits in yourself, no matter what money fears plague you, no matter what investment personality type you are?

FOUR TRAITS OF A GOOD INVESTOR
In our years of advising friends and clients, we've seen four traits again and again in the people who achieve the most financial success.

People with these four traits tend to make sound money decisions throughout their lives, even when their circumstances change. They show self-control. They're able to wait when that's the best course of action, and willing to act when the time is right. They have the realistic self-confidence of the Balanced investment personality that we discussed in the previous chapter.

1. Organization
We can't stress enough the importance of good organization. Being organized is a trait that will serve you well your entire life, and not just in money matters.

Being organized means having a filing system, keeping receipts, and recording details. It means creating a budget and keeping a financial journal. We'll tell you how to do all those things in Chapter 4. Having a system for keeping track of your information and your money will save you hours, days, even weeks when you need to access the information.

Many people are surprised, positively or negatively, to learn where they actually stand once they get themselves organized.

2. Discipline

Chances are, much of your life revolves around discipline. You wake up to an alarm clock, stop at red lights, show up for work on time, study and finish homework, remember birthdays, learn new skills, and do a variety of other things that require you to follow life's large and small rules.

There are rules and best practices around money too. Growing up, you may have learned the basics of what money is and how to spend it. But unless you read a book on investing or took a course in financial planning, you may not know a lot beyond that.

Learning to follow money rules and practices isn't much different from learning to plant a garden. Do you have the discipline to do the ground work? Are you willing to stick with your plan, to follow through on your goals? Do you have a contingency plan if things go wrong? Have you planted a well-balanced mix? Are you open to a professional's advice?

3. Patience

Many people buy a stock or invest in a fund and hope it will rise at once. They think that just because they bought it, it should be ready to jump. If the investment doesn't go up immediately, they sell and move on to another that looks more promising. That's a mistake.

Be patient. It takes not only discipline but patience to hold good investments, stay focused on your goals, and follow a financial plan.

Think of patience as concentrated strength. When things get tough, it's easy to abandon your plan, sell off your portfolio, and sit on cash. It's harder to take your financial advisor's advice to stay the course. Don't sell a great stock because it hasn't risen in the time frame you imagined. Great companies do well over time—the key words being *over time*. Those who have good investments and patience are rewarded in the end.

4. Good habits

We often ask clients whose net worth is several million dollars how they got where they are. It's usually not because they won the lottery or came into huge inheritances, but because they consistently practised good habits.

Good habits are hard to create. Have you noticed? It's hard to get to the gym three times a week. It's hard to eat as many vegetables as you should. It's hard to floss every single night. And it's really hard to get into the habit of saving your money or paying down debt. But the habit of saving is one that will benefit you and your family over a lifetime.

Many of our wealthy clients aren't that different from you. They simply did things the right way, with some sort of order or strategy. They got organized, budgeted, examined their net worth, and made a financial plan. Often they started small, buying a modest home that appreciated smartly over time, as many assets do. And they were disciplined. When money came in, they paid themselves first, making mortgage payments and contributing to their retirement plans. Some chose a mortgage with a 20-year or even 15-year amortization instead of the standard 25. That meant higher monthly payments, but their home was paid off five to ten years earlier.

When you pay yourself first, you finish first. It's amazing what a few hundred dollars here and there can do when you put it to work instead of splurging on your wardrobe or the spa. It takes work to save money, and it takes really good habits. If you establish those habits, you'll be well on your way to financial success.

NATURE VERSUS NURTURE

Do you have the traits of a good investor? Are you naturally self-disciplined and patient? Do you find it easy to stick to good habits? If so, congratulations. You're in a strong position to take control of your financial future. We'll tell you exactly how to do that through the rest of this book.

What if most or all of the traits are foreign to you? What if you're terrible at saving money? Or you're the Spontaneous investment personality type? Or money fears are holding you back? Is there anything you can do?

Stanford University's late-1960s "marshmallow test" is one of the most famous studies of people's natural tendency toward patience or impulsivity. In the test, a researcher presented preschoolers with one marshmallow and told them they'd get a second marshmallow if they did not eat the first but waited a few minutes. Then the researcher left the room.

What happened? Some children couldn't resist temptation; they gobbled their marshmallow at once. Some held out for a while but still ate the marshmallow before the researcher returned. And some were able to wait until the researcher came back 15 to 20 minutes later. Although it was difficult, these children recognized that by delaying their gratification, they'd achieve the goal of two marshmallows.

The Stanford study tracked these same children over many years. Later in life, those who'd waited for their second marshmallow had more fulfilling careers, higher incomes, more successful marriages, better health, and other achievements that suggested they were happier than the children who'd pounced on the first marshmallow. What's more, they were better able to focus their attention, check their impulses, prioritize, and stick to a plan. These, as we've said, are traits closely linked to money management skills.

So if you're impulsive by nature, are you out of luck? Are the traits that make up your money personality fixed for life?

Recent research says no: Delayed gratification doesn't have to be hard-wired; it can be learned. In 2012, researchers at the University of Rochester duplicated the marshmallow test but made an important change. They subjected one group of children to reliable experiences— if the children waited, they got the promised reward—and a second group to unreliable experiences—even if they waited, they never got the reward.

Bit by bit, the first group retrained their brains to understand that waiting paid off. In fact, by the end of the study, the first group of children waited on average four times longer than the second for their reward. This showed researchers that, as with gardening, environment matters. Nurture, not just nature, shapes the ability to delay gratification in favour of a bigger payoff down the road.

Even if you're not naturally a self-disciplined, patient person, you can become more that way. You can train your brain by adopting and practising new behaviours that will make you better at planning, saving, and reaching sound investment decisions.

In the rest of this book, we'll show you exactly what those behaviours are. We'll show you how to get organized, plan your financial garden, plant the right investments, and reap your rewards.

Jasmine's bony elbow in her side made Rose jump. "What did I tell you? Not bad for an old dude, right?"

"He's hardly old." Rose stole a glance at Tripp, who was working to one side of the front cash, loading the last of the houseplants onto a dolly. He had pushed the long sleeves of his T-shirt up, she noticed, and he moved fluidly, a man comfortable in his own skin. She was staring, she suddenly realized, and wrenched her gaze back to Jasmine. "He's probably younger than me."

"Old-*er*, then," said Jasmine. "If I was single and of your, like, generation, I wouldn't chase him away."

"Enough, already." Rose lowered her voice. "You know, every time a guy over a certain age comes in here, you try to set me up. I've told you, I'm done with men. I'm okay being on my own."

Jasmine lifted one eyebrow. It was a move she'd mastered. "Uh-huh. Whatever." The girl rooted through the long knitted bag that served as her purse. "Listen, can I borrow twenty bucks? That juice bar I'm going to tonight—"

"Again? You still owe me ten."

"I know. Just till Friday. I'll pay it all back then."

Rose shoved a box of plastic bags under the counter and considered how much to say. It's not like she was the girl's mother. "Why not skip the juice bar if you can't afford it? Eat at home instead?"

Jasmine laughed. "Not a chance. Everyone's tried that place except me. Besides, I'm meeting Sadie there. Then we're going downtown, probably hit the reggae club. Come on, Rosie. You know I'm good for it."

Rose knew. It might take weeks, but Jasmine always paid her back. Still, she worried about the girl, house-sitting one month, couch-surfing the next, living paycheque to paycheque, busking for spare change with her beat-up guitar whenever the Blooming Tulip wasn't busy enough to give her a shift. It's all an adventure when you're twenty, but what about five years from now? Ten?

Who are you to criticize? There it was again, the soundtrack of Laurel. *Like you had any money of your own when Dad left. You let him do it all, manage the accounts, pay your bills. He gave you an allowance. An allowance! Like you were a kid.*

It was true. Rose never had a head for numbers, and Frank was an accountant, after all. It made sense for him to look after the money—once they had some. In the early years, while he was still in school, there were times when they could barely make rent. She'd had to borrow a twenty or two in her day, especially once the happy surprise of Laurel came along.

She glanced at Jasmine, who was smiling dreamily. The girl seemed happy the way she was. Rose reached under the counter for her purse and dug out a twenty.

4

Where You Are

Laurel glanced at the travel alarm clock she kept on the bathroom counter and took a deep breath as she stepped out of the shower. One hour to date time. Right on schedule.

After towelling dry and applying a vanilla-and-honey-scented moisturizer, she faced the mirror. Not bad for a thirty-two-year-old mother of two. Complexion a little blotchy, but foundation would fix it. Still toned and trim, thanks to a workout schedule that seemed harder to keep up with all the time. Rough heels and unpolished toenails—ugh, could she squeeze a pedicure out of next month's carefully planned budget? Decent haircut, chin-length, layered. If only she could splurge on highlights like in the double-income days when Matthew was alive.

Matthew. After three years, the thought of him still hurt like a punch to the gut.

You'll get over it, people used to say back when it was fresh. You'll get over it, the support group leader told her a year later. You'll get over it, Mom said gently on those rare occasions now when Laurel admitted how deeply, in the very core of her being, she still missed her husband.

Really? She wanted to scream at them all. I'll get over it? We planned our whole lives together, and two months shy of his thirtieth birthday some drunk runs a red light in his midlife-crisis sports car and sends the love of my life, the father of my twins, flying halfway down the block, and I'm supposed to get over it?

She pulled a brush through her wet hair, yanking at every snarl, counting on the pain to remind her that this was her life, now, today. Get a grip, she told herself. The pity party stops now. Greg is the best lead you've had in months. He sounds great onscreen, even greater on the phone. There might be something there this time. Don't blow it.

YOUR FINANCIAL LANDSCAPE

Before you plant a garden, you need to understand the land. Is it rocky or level? Does it need tilling and enrichment? Is the soil too acidic? Too sandy?

Before you take control of your financial future, you need to know what your personal landscape looks like. Where are you today? Where would you like to be? And where—with a goal, a plan, some effort, and some common sense—might you realistically be tomorrow?

This chapter will help you determine your starting point and your goal. But first, ask yourself a few questions.

Why am I reading this book?

We think you're reading these words not only to learn more about personal finance but also to improve your financial position. Most people we know would like to be better off than they are.

We want to demystify money for you, and we want you to feel proud of what you achieve. They say that effort is its own reward, but tangibles sure do help. Our advice for financial planning is based on the assumption that you'd like to build your wealth over time.

How do I feel about money?

People grow up believing all sorts of things about money, and those beliefs can become deeply internalized. What were you raised to believe? Was money considered good or evil? Did it lead to panic and anxiety? A fear of poverty? A sense of abundance and joy? Maybe you consider the love of money to be the root of all evil.

Consider this: Money is neither good nor bad. It's simply a means of expressing value. Money can mean a car, a facelift, a finished basement, an education. It can mean a new well in Rwanda, a roof over your child's head, a smart little sailboat, relief for victims of disaster or war. Ludwig von Mises, noted economist and social philosopher, put it this way: "Economics is not about goods and services; it is about human choice and action."

Does money intimidate me?

If you feel that money has power over you, the idea of making a financial plan may feel scary.

Think about your money for a minute. Remember, it's *yours*. You earned it, and you're the person who decides where it should go, whether to a savings account or a credit card bill. Did you really need everything you bought last month? Could you have done without some of it? That money could even have become the seed funding for an investment account.

Money should not have power over you. You have power over it. You did the work and made the decisions that created that money. The more you accumulate, the more decisions you'll make along the way, and the easier those decisions will become.

What would I like to change about my financial life?

Imagine what you could do if you were debt-free. With no monthly payments to worry about, you could make your money work for you rather than making others wealthy by passing your money straight into their pockets.

Allow yourself to dream about your perfect financial life. What does financial success look like to you? What has to happen, and what has to change, for you to get there?

Rose poured a glass of chardonnay and sank onto Laurel's sofa. It had taken an hour and a half to get the twins settled. First the rubber duck battle in the tub. Then the towel fight in the bedroom. Then, when they were finally friends again (weren't twins supposed to get along?), the three, count 'em three, stories she had to read before the boys' eyelids finally drooped.

How does Laurel do it? Rose took a cool sip of wine. Keep two young hooligans in check and cart them around between school and soccer and karate and work fifty-hour weeks and manage a household and manage her mother's finances (though not so much now, Rose was getting the hang of it) and still stay sane?

For all that she'd been the one to push Laurel, squalling and beet-faced, into this world, Rose had always found the girl a mystery. Laurel was Frank's daughter in every way, from her boundless energy to her iron discipline to her career as a corporate accountant. She was Frank's, too, in her inability to relax and just have fun. I'm focusing, was Frank's usual reply when Rose tapped on his study door in the evenings to ask if he'd go for a walk with her or join her in a cup of tea. You're boring, Rose wanted to shoot back, though she never had the guts to.

Hopefully Laurel was having fun tonight. As weary as Rose felt after the tumultuous day at work, she hoped Laurel wouldn't creep in until the wee hours. Her steel-willed daughter was good at so many things, yet Rose worried about her. Since Matthew's death, Laurel's life had become a gruelling treadmill that seemed to run her instead of the other way around. She worked and worked, but for what? There were precious few rewards in her life, apart from the boys, who on some days were more challenge than reward.

Something had to change.

Change . . . it was in the air. Rose's mind drifted back over the day. A new owner, a new direction for the garden centre. And Tripp.

From the moment she'd seen him, she couldn't get the new landscaper out of her head. And she was furious at herself. So he was startlingly handsome and his shirt fit him well. So what? Good-looking men were a dime a dozen. So he'd gazed at her that way, levelly, with those eyes, as if he'd seen something both surprising and instantly familiar. So what?

So a jolt had sliced through her when she touched his hand. So what?

She didn't need to be vulnerable. Not again.

———

We hope we've got you thinking about taking control of your money, growing it, and using it to achieve your dreams.

As we said earlier, the first step in planning where to go is to understand where you are right now. To figure that out, you'll need to do three things.

1. Get organized

In Chapter 3, we said that organization is one of the four traits of a good investor. Organizing your financial life is one of the most important things you can do. It takes time now, but it will save you huge amounts of time later, when you need to get at information. Being organized is one of the best financial habits you can develop.

2. Make a budget

A budget will put you in control of your financial life. It's empowering to be in charge instead of at the mercy of every whim. A budget will also help you decide if what you're currently doing is what you really should be doing, or if you should make some changes. And if you routinely have more month than money? Don't panic. We'll suggest some ways to fix that.

3. Determine your personal net worth

Your net worth is the difference between what you own and what you owe. If you've never calculated it before, you may be in for a surprise. Knowing your net worth gives you a snapshot of where you are financially at this very moment. As we've said, you need to know that before you can plan where you want to go in the future.

Getting organized, making a budget, and determining your net worth are the hardest things we'll ask you to do in this book. Once you've finished, you'll have a much better understanding of what your money can do for you, and you'll be ready to put that understanding into action. Knowing what you have right now, as well as your potential for the future, will ease you through the remaining steps to financial success.

If you've completed these three steps before, great. You're well ahead of the game. Use this chapter to review your information and make sure it's still current.

GET ORGANIZED

Action item: Do this step now. Don't put it off. Getting down to business in a businesslike way will help you feel more organized and *be* more organized.

First, gather up your key financial documents:

- Income tax returns
- Statements for your chequing and savings accounts, credit cards, mortgage, loans, and credit lines
- Property assessments
- Investment statements
- Pension reports (or statements giving your projected income at retirement)

The list may seem daunting, but you'll need these items to determine your income, make your budget and calculate your net worth.

Second, figure out how and where to store your documents. Get yourself a filing cabinet or large box and some file folders. Resist the out-of-sight, out-of-mind urge to stuff everything into a box under the bed. Your documents have to be easy to find when you need them. If you're overwhelmed by the amount of paper, consider online options.

We recommend that you store your most precious documents—passports, birth certificates, certificates of marital status, and so on—in a safe deposit box at the bank or in a locked, fire-resistant home safe.

Third, start a financial journal. It should be user-friendly, ideally something you can tuck into a briefcase or purse that you regularly carry. You may want a coil-bound notebook that lies flat when opened. Or you may prefer a laptop or tablet. Find what works for you and what you're most comfortable using. You'll use the journal for taking notes and recording ideas. We'll talk more about that in Chapter 5.

Lulled by the quiet—the twins were finally, truly asleep—and a top-up of chardonnay, Rose drifted, her mind a strange mixture of tired and wired.

Don't think about that Tripp person, she told herself. Don't do it. She focused on mundane things instead, what she'd have for breakfast, errands that had piled up, the handyman who was coming to her apartment tomorrow to price a bathroom reno. Well, partial reno—tearing out the old green tub and replacing it with a glass-enclosed shower, rainhead fixture and all.

After almost a year in her shabby condo—the Seventies Museum, Laurel called it—Rose had the handyman's phone number memorized. Bit by bit, she was trying to nudge the place into the 21st century with her limited budget. Most days it felt as if she'd hardly made it to the eighties. The two-bedroom apartment, with its stippled ceilings, vinyl flooring, and palette of autumn gold and avocado green, was an embarrassing contrast to the beautifully decorated Cape Cod she'd called home before the divorce.

Of course, money and time were both plentiful back then. Frank owned his own accounting firm, so she never needed a job. Once Laurel had descended into the Hades of her teenage years, when she'd rather have her fingernails yanked out than be seen anywhere with her mother, Rose threw herself into projects. She redecorated the house, redid the yard, and then, having developed a feel for soil, immersed herself in courses on horticulture and landscaping. That led to her Master Gardener designation and years of volunteering for any family member, friend, or neighbour who needed a green thumb.

That's what Tripp will be doing for Blooming Tulip clients, she thought. Though doing it for money, and with those arms....

No, no, no. Rose pushed herself off the sofa and paced around Laurel's big living room. She wouldn't do it. She wouldn't think about that man.

Not after a year of getting her life together, a whole year of figuring out how to live on her own, trying to manage her own financial affairs, how to be her own woman.

MAKE A BUDGET

Like Rose, many women know what they earn but have no idea where their money goes. Knowing how, and on what, you spend your money is an essential step in determining where you are. It may prompt you to make some serious changes.

Once you've gathered your financial documents, you're ready to draw up a budget. If you aren't sure how to do this, use the sample budget at the end of this chapter. You can tailor the sample by adding or subtracting categories to match your own situation. There are also lots of free budget spreadsheets and worksheets available online, often on bank websites.

Some financial gurus talk about keeping track of your daily, weekly, monthly, and yearly budget, but that's a lot of work. (And our sample budget doesn't give you enough room to record all that.) Use monthly figures throughout your budget. That will make it easier to track expenses in particular, since many bills come in monthly.

If you're not sure of a monthly amount, take the annual amount (if you know it) and divide by 12. Or take the daily amount and multiply by 30.

Income

In the income category, write down your work income and any other money you receive regularly. Include occasional amounts as long as getting them is an expected occurrence. You can record your income before tax if that's easier, as long as you deduct taxes later. The sample budget reminds you to do that.

If your income is variable—if you work on commission, for example—make an educated guess and correct the figure when you know your exact income. A variable income can make budgeting more challenging, but it can also bring pleasant surprises, giving you the chance to add a little extra to your savings or investments.

Savings

In the savings category, write down the monthly amounts you put into a savings account, retirement fund, education fund, emergency fund, or other safe parking place.

What *about* those savings? Are you putting money aside into various funds? Saving is such an important step to financial success that we cover it in depth in Chapter 5. There, we'll show you how even a small amount of money will grow over the years. The figures are amazing. The sooner you start saving, the more money you'll have, so be sure to include some savings in your monthly budget.

Saving for a vacation, retirement, or education (your own or a child's) can be fun. You have something to look forward to at the end. But it's just as important to save for the less fun things in life, many of which are hard to predict. Who knew you'd have to replace your ancient fridge during a heat wave? Who knew the dog would need a $500 veterinary bill? Who knew your throbbing tooth would lead to an expensive root canal? For these and other unpredictable outlays, you need to set aside a little something each month as an emergency fund.

Expenses

Now plug your regular monthly expenses into your budget. These may include mortgage or rent, electricity, heat, cable, credit card bills, cell phone, and so on. You're used to paying these bills straight off the top of your income; putting them in your budget makes them even easier to remember.

Clients often tell us their budget got derailed by an unexpected expense. When we ask what it was, the answer is car insurance or property tax or tuition. Sure, those expenses may not come up every month, but they're not unexpected. You have to budget for your annual outlays. Divide the expense by twelve, then set that much aside every month until the item comes due. Seeing the amount in your budget each month will remind you to set the money aside. Then those big—but predictable—expenditures won't catch you by surprise.

How can you make sure the money you set aside stays aside? Open a dedicated savings account. You'll be less tempted to rob the piggy bank if you have a separate account for your annual expenditures. When it's time to pay the bill, you won't need to scramble—the money will be right there because you deposited one-twelfth of it every month.

You'll also have a lot of daily and weekly expenses. We're talking about things like groceries, toiletries, babysitting, meals out, tickets to special events, and all the "chump change" that slips through your fingers when you aren't looking.

These expenditures will vary. The best thing is to bite the bullet and spend two or three weeks recording them. (Your financial journal is the perfect place for this.) You'll soon get an idea of your average outlay for daily and weekly items. Convert the amounts into monthly totals and put them in your budget. You shouldn't have to recalculate the amounts unless something major affects your spending.

You'll notice that over a week, a month, a year, daily spending on small items like lunch out or a latte (or three) really adds up. If you can afford these little luxuries, or they give you a chance to schmooze with your co-workers or take a break from the office, by all means make room for them in your budget. But if you're horrified by the totals, and realize that your coffee shop bill equals a trip to Mexico, you may decide to adjust your spending. Adding up the small expenses is one of the most eye-opening steps of making a budget.

Once you've recorded all the expenses you can think of, subtract them from your income. What's left is your *disposable income*. If your disposable income is a positive number, you're living within your means. If it's negative, you'll have to make some adjustments if you hope to move forward. Here's where the sample budget's Need and Want columns come into play.

Need and want

The term *budget* scares a lot of people. They consider it a restriction, but it really isn't. A budget is a plan for what you *can* spend, not what you can't. A budget allows you to concentrate on what will bring you the highest rewards (your short-term needs) while getting you closer to your goals (your long-term needs and greatest wants).

The money you spend each month falls into two categories: Need and Want. When you first look over your budget, you'll probably think most of your expenses belong in the Need column. Of course, some budgeted items are a must. You need a roof over your head; you need food; you need some kind of phone. But after a couple of tries, you can probably shift many expenses into the Want column without making your life miserable.

As your habits change, Need and Want will guide your spending. Without getting crazy about it, you'll start to think twice about your grocery, clothing, and other purchases, small and large. Do you really need a second e-reader? Is a luxury car really necessary to get you where you're going? Is buying a huge house instead of a modest one the right thing to do on your salary? We're not saying don't buy these things—that's your decision. We're just asking you to think about whether the purchase is a Need or a Want.

When you think about your expenditures, savings should always come first. Consider savings a Need. If you pay yourself first and live off the rest, it will help you build for the future. Saving money and progressing toward your goals—which we'll talk about more in Chapter 5—will give you peace of mind and a feeling of independence and satisfaction.

Where are you now?

The money that goes in and out of your pocket is called *cash flow*. One of the easiest and best ways to understand your cash flow is to examine your personal budget.

How do your numbers look? Is your disposable income positive or negative? If it's positive, and you're living within your means, that's great. You'll have more means to work with in the future. If, however, you're spending more than you make, you're going backwards. No matter where you are now, if you're going backwards you'll need to look seriously at your situation.

If your budget shows you're spending too freely, take a hard look at the Need and Want columns. Which items can you shift over to Want? Which can you get rid of altogether? Are there any items that you could buy less often, that could become occasional treats instead of regular pleasures?

If you're sensible about your spending but don't have enough income, you have choices. Can you get a higher-paying job? Work a second job part-time? Improve your education? Work from home some or all of the time and spend less on commuting, wardrobe, lunches out, and so on?

Wherever you stand, if you don't like what your budget tells you, you can change things. Remember, you are in control of your money, not the other way around. Your earnings, savings, and expenses are key factors in determining not just where you are now and where you'll be in the future, but also where you can be if you make some adjustments to what you're doing now.

We urge you to be sensible and take small steps. Spending and saving are like pruning. Done right, trimming a bit here and there will stimulate your garden's growth. Done wrong, it will stunt your plants. If you get rid of everything, including next year's seeds, you'll eventually have no blooms. If you cut too much from your budget, you may make yourself miserable.

We also urge you to look at your budget regularly. Tuck a paper copy inside your financial journal so that it's easy to find. And don't forget to update your budget as your situation changes. An outdated budget isn't very useful. It's a picture of where you *were*, not where you are.

DETERMINE YOUR NET WORTH

Having a budget, as we've said, helps you monitor your cash flow—what comes in and what goes out. Knowing your net worth, or what you've accumulated, helps you create a longer-term plan.

All successful money managers have a plan to guide them. (We'll talk more about building your plan in Chapter 5.) Without a plan, you run risks, like spending most of what you have and ending up impoverished in the future. In that future, especially when your work income stops, your net worth will help fund your lifestyle. That's why you need to get a handle on what you're worth today.

As with getting organized and making your personal budget, determining your net worth takes some work. But it will pay off. Think of it as planting seeds for your life in bloom.

The best place to record your net worth is your financial journal. On a clean page, write down the headings "What I Own" and "What I Owe." Then list all the major items you can think of under each heading. Your list might look something like this:

What I Own

- Car
- Condo
- Collection of original art

What I Owe

- Car loan
- Mortgage
- Line of credit

Now put a value beside each category. Your car might be worth $15,000. Your car loan might be $10,000.

Keep going. Walk around your home and write down the major items you own and their values. Don't worry about small things, like clothes, books, or basic personal belongings. Keep doing this until you've listed and valued everything of significance inside and outside your home.

It's a great idea, as well, to photograph your valuables as you list them. Photos are an important record for insurance purposes.

Now grab a calculator. Add up everything in the Own column, then everything in the Owe column. Subtract one from each other. The result is your net worth—what you own, minus what you owe.

Is your net worth positive? Wonderful. You're off to a great start. Your financial plan will involve increasing that net worth further to strengthen your position for the future.

Is your net worth negative? Do you have few assets? Too many debts? Your financial plan will focus on getting you into positive territory, then building from there.

———⊗⊗⊗———

By now, you should have a much clearer picture of where you are. Is your garden just beginning to grow? Is it already blooming beautifully? Is it drooping from neglect? Your personal financial landscape will depend on a number of variables.

One is your age. If you're young, and just starting a career and getting established, your budget may be tight and your net worth small, even negative. If you're into your 40s, 50s, or 60s, you're probably earning more money than ever. You may own a home and have a retirement plan or a pension. You probably have more disposable income, making it easier to save, invest, and accumulate wealth.

Your investment personality and money habits are other important variables, as we discussed in Chapters 2 and 3. How you personally feel about, approach, and handle money plays a big role in where you are today.

Now that you know more about who you are and where you are, you're ready to think about your financial future. Your map to that future is your step-by-step financial plan. We'll talk about planning, and the five steps to financial success, in the next chapter.

———⊗⊗⊗———

That's it, I'm done, Laurel vowed. That was my last Internet date. She swung her SUV out of the parking garage and into the nighttime downtown traffic. In the back seat, a soccer ball rolled to one side, hitting the door with a soft thunk.

In the early days, certain that the only way she'd ever make herself date again was to turn it into a project, she had logged the numbers: how many contacts, how many follow-up texts and calls, how many first dates, second dates, and so on. "What do you expect?" she'd asked her friend Jenny, who had laughed out loud at her meticulous Excel file. "I'm an accountant." But six months later, she quit keeping track. The numbers only depressed her. There were no third dates, for example. Not one.

Over and over, the same thing. They'd butter her up—pull out her chair, scatter compliments, say they liked her voice or her hair or some other inconsequential thing. Then the evening went one of two ways. Door number one: they'd fixate on her job. Are there many women accountants out there? Don't you find it boring sometimes? You must do pretty well for yourself. Know how copper wire was invented? Two accountants fighting over a penny. Door number two: they'd fixate on themselves. Either way, Laurel ended things fast. No way was she putting valuable time into a bad investment.

She'd had such high hopes for tonight. Greg had sounded different, sincere, interesting. Yet dinner had started so predictably that she'd almost turned around and left. Greg said she looked beautiful (yeah, right) and that he'd been so excited about meeting her that he hadn't slept the night before (sure). After a few more compliments (rehearsed, no doubt), he asked about her work (here we go).

Around the time they'd finished their appetizers, right on schedule, Greg began to talk about himself, his job as partner in an immigration law firm, his passion for cycling, his retro collection of record albums. Door number two, she decided: fixated on himself.

Then things took a turn. He asked her what she thought about some change to the immigration law. She hadn't heard about the change or the debate leading up to it, so had nothing to say. Then he asked her about music. Who did she listen to nowadays? She cast around for a name, any name, before opting for honesty: she didn't have time to listen to music. He described touring the south of France, his favourite cycling trip ever. Had she been there? Never been to Europe, she admitted. It was impossible to travel, what with the kids and work.

Greg sipped more wine, looked at her kindly. What did she do for fun, then? Besides work and the kids, what were her passions? Her dreams?

The traffic light turned green and Laurel stomped the accelerator. She wanted to get home. *Home.* The boys would be asleep, flung out on their beds like starfish. Her mother would have dozed off on the sofa. The alarm would be set for five-thirty so Laurel could do the workout she'd missed today because of the deluge of email. Her home, her family, her schedule. The familiar routine closed tight around her and comforted her.

She had felt stupid with Greg, stammering non-answers to all his questions. Stupid and . . . something else, something she couldn't put her finger on. Whatever it was, she didn't like it. And she didn't like him for making her feel that way. Who did he think he was anyway, pumping her for so many personal details on a first date? How was she supposed to have— what was it he said?—passions and dreams? She had too much to *do.*

Greg had looked at her hopefully when they said good-night, hopefully and tentatively. She knew that look. It said, Will there be another date?

No way. The soccer ball thunked again as she took a corner fast. With one arm, she felt around behind the seat, trying to contain the loose ball. I'm done.

CATEGORY	AMOUNT	NEED	WANT
Income			
Employment income and bonus			
Interest income			
Investment income			
Rental income			
Miscellaneous income			
Income subtotal			
Taxes			
Income taxes deducted			
Savings			
Retirement			
Savings account			
University/college			
Emergency fund			
Net Income (Income minus taxes and savings)			
Expenses			
Household Expenses			
Mortgage payment			
Rent payment			
Property tax			

Maintenance fees			
Utilities			
Food			
Groceries			
Restaurants/coffee shops			
Family Expenses			
Children's activities			
Child support/alimony			
Day care/babysitting/preschool			
Health Care			
Insurance			
Fitness equipment/yoga/gym membership			
Prescription drugs/other medications			
Prosthetics/orthotics			
Chiropractor/naturopath/physiotherapist/massage therapist			
Dental			
Eyewear			
Transportation			
Car payments			
Gasoline			
Repairs/maintenance			
Insurance			
Other (tolls/buses/subways/taxis/parking)			
Debt Payments			

Credit cards			
Student loans			
Credit lines			
Other loans			
Entertainment			
Internet/cable			
Hobbies			
Magazines/books			
Vacations			
Pets			
Food			
Grooming/obedience classes			
Veterinarian fees			
Clothing			
Miscellaneous			
Toiletries/household products			
Gifts/donations			
Grooming (hair/nails/cosmetics)			
Other			
Expenses subtotal			
Disposable Income			
(total income minus total expenses)			

Part Two: Planting

5

Your Financial Success

"Here's your money," Jasmine said. "Well, some of it."

Rose felt something scrape her palm, looked down at a crumpled ten-dollar bill. "You weren't going to pay me back until Friday."

"I got lucky." Jasmine's cheeks dimpled. "Someone I met at the juice bar last night picked up the tab. For me *and* Sadie. Came with us to the reggae club too and paid the whole shot."

Rose smiled. "You're blushing."

"Am not!"

Several sharp claps rang out from the front of the garden centre. It was Mrs. Birch. They were closing early today, she had announced at noon. An impromptu staff meeting to round out the day. Now it was time, and a couple of workers strolled over to her.

Rose wiped her hands on her stained khakis. "So you found yourself a sugar daddy."

"No." With a well-scuffed toe, Jasmine kicked at a fallen fuchsia blossom. A moment passed. "I never said *daddy*."

"Oh, okay. I see." Rose glanced up front. He wasn't there yet.

"Do you—" Jasmine looked up, shoulders hunched, kohl-rimmed eyes wide. "I mean, what do you think about that?"

"Pffft." Rose waved a hand, as if batting a fly. "Daddy, mama. Who cares? It's the sugar part you're desperately in need of."

Jasmine relaxed and grinned. "Tell me about it. I need new safety shoes real soon. But look, this person, it's nothing serious. At least not yet. I'm just, you know, curious. About what the options are."

Rose scanned the front again. More staff had gathered, but not him.

"He's going to be late," said Jasmine. "I overheard him telling Mrs. Birch."

"Who?" It was Rose's turn to blush. "I mean, why do you . . ."

"Are you serious? Ever since the guy strolled in here yesterday, you're like—" Jasmine swivelled her head from side to side, exaggerating cartoonishly. "You follow him around. With your eyes."

Rose wanted to contradict the girl but words escaped her. "Come on," she said instead. "The meeting's about to start."

PLANNING MATTERS

With a garden, if you merely scatter a few seeds and walk away, you won't have much to show in the end. For your garden to flourish, you have to decide ahead of time what to plant and where to plant it. Then you have to nurture what you sow, feeding what's desirable, weeding out what isn't, keeping an eye on the weather.

The same goes for your money. A scattered approach typically means scattered results. To make your financial garden bloom, you need to set goals, then build a realistic plan that will lead you, step by step, toward those goals.

Take retirement, for example. When we ask clients what their lives will be like when they retire, many aren't sure. They have no specific plan for what they're going to do. They may have an age in mind—say 55, 60, or 65—but they don't know if they can realistically hit that goal. When we ask what it costs them to live now, they often don't know. If you don't know how much you need now, how can you gauge what you'll need after you retire?

Having read this far, you're well on your way toward building a plan. You've organized yourself, made a personal budget, and determined your net worth. That means you know where you are. Now you're ready to plant your financial success, to chart your course for the future.

This chapter calls on you to visualize what that future might be in a more specific way than you did earlier, then figure out how to get there. In Chapter 1, we said you'd be taking some small but bold steps to make your dreams come true. The time to take those steps is now.

FIVE STEPS TO FINANCIAL SUCCESS

- Begin at the beginning
- Set goals

- Find clarity
- Segue into savings
- Build your personal financial plan

Step 1: Begin at the beginning

The work you did in Chapter 4 gave you great insight into where you are right now. You'll need to think further about your budget and net worth now, so keep that information handy.

On a clean page of your financial journal, write: "What do I want to change in my financial life?"

Jot down your answers. Go into as much detail as you need. The answers are yours and yours alone. You'll find that the physical act of writing down what you'd like to change will help program your brain for success.

On another clean page, write: "What does financial success look like to me?"

Take your time with this question. Sit by yourself in a quiet place. Relax and let your mind drift. This is the page for dreaming your future.

Imagine your *perfect financial life*. Make your dream as big as you want. It can be a solid, practical dream, or something airy and abstract. Write down whatever you envision. After all, if you don't know what success means to you, how can you achieve it?

Some people find it helpful to flip through magazines and cut out images of what they'd like to see in their perfect lives. Assembling a collage of those images into a dream board or scrapbook is a useful way of visualizing life as you want it to be.

Step 2: Set goals

In Step 1, by asking you to visualize and write down what financial success looks like to you, we took you to the heart of your goals. Now, on another clean page, write: "What barriers are standing in my way?" Jot down anything that comes to mind.

Then write: "What's a creative way of getting rid of each barrier?" As you eliminate barriers, you'll be giving yourself permission to set the long-term goals you've dreamed about.

You may discover that short-term goals will help you reach your longer-term goals. Say, for example, that you'd really like a more satisfying job, and what's standing in your way is your level of education. Maybe you need to work *extra hours* to earn *extra money* so you can *hire a babysitter* while you *go back to school* so you can get a more satisfying job. Achieving your long-term goal of a more satisfying job involves four short-term goals along the way.

Now, write each goal on a separate page of your journal. For each goal, write down your ideas for how to make it specific, realistic, and at-tainable—in other words, how to make it come true. Start each idea with "I commit to . . ." That will help you later, when you ask yourself whether your ideas are realistic and attainable. The trick to making dreams come true is to find specific strategies you can actually follow.

Your detailed strategies for each goal may require extra pages. That's fine. Don't skimp on space or try to shorten this process.

A big question to answer for each goal is *when?* Remember that some-day isn't a day of the week. Deadlines and target dates matter.

Here's an example to get you started: "I want to be mortgage-free by age 65."

That's a great goal with a clear deadline. Here's how to add specifics:

- I commit to talking to my banker about ways to pay off my mortgage more quickly.
- I commit to putting an extra $50 from each paycheque toward my mortgage.
- I commit to spending less by buying one less latte a day.
- I commit to taking in a boarder who will pay me rent that I'll apply to my mortgage.
- I commit to ensuring that the amortization period left on my mortgage doesn't go past my 65th birthday.
- I commit to asking for a raise at work and applying the increase to the principal of my mortgage.

If your goal still looks unattainable, you may need a tougher course of action:

- I commit to looking for a better, higher-paying job in keeping with my skills and education.
- I commit to getting retraining or more education.
- I commit to selling my house and buying a less expensive place.

To iron out some details and set a realistic time frame for meeting your financial goals, you may need the help of a professional, like the banker mentioned above. In Chapter 6, we'll show you how to build the team you need. For now, on your own, do exactly as we've suggested for all your goals. Write down all the things you can do to overcome the barriers to your goals and help you achieve them.

Now go back and ask yourself if you *can* and *will* realistically do all these things. Can you truly commit to them? Maybe you don't have room to take in a boarder, or housing someone isn't your idea of fun. Scratch that idea off the list. Maybe you're already at the top of your pay scale, so a raise isn't in the cards. And so it goes, until you're left with the ideas that are realistic and attainable.

⁓

They were having what Mrs. Birch called a stand-up meeting. "Trust me, you stand up and the meeting moves along," she told them. "You sit down and things drag on forever. We don't have that kind of time."

Their new boss had run through the schedule for the garden centre's closing and grand reopening a week later. She had assigned everyone an area they'd be responsible for during the shutdown and outlined their main tasks. Fifteen minutes in, the sliding doors had whooshed open and in walked Tripp. Dark denim shirt, Rose noted. It turned his eyes cobalt.

By the half-hour mark, a few people had started to fidget. "Okay, everyone, change of pace." Mrs. Birch stood taller and raised one arm, a conductor about to lower the baton. All motion stopped. Wow, thought Rose. Rumour was, Mrs. Birch had turned around twelve companies in the last two decades, and had come close to making the Forbes Most Powerful Women list. It was easy to see why.

"Dreams," Mrs. Birch said. "I want to hear your dreams. If you could do anything with this place, anything at all, what would it be?"

⁓

Step 3: Find clarity
Life is never static. When circumstances change, you need to change too.

Say you come into a sudden windfall or get hit with a major expense. Suddenly your financial picture is out of focus. What should you do? Spend more, save more, give to charity, get a loan—what? Having specific goals and a solid plan will give you the clarity you need to stay on top of your affairs.

We have a friend whose line of credit was like a weedy jungle. The principal started off low, and the monthly interest payment was modest. As her debt climbed, the interest grew out of control. She needed to pay down the line of credit, but how? Going through her budget line by line, we identified several unnecessary expenses that totalled over $600 a month. With her overspending laid bare, our friend found cheaper but satisfying alternatives that enabled her to stick to her plan to pay down her debt. Her budget and financial plan gave her clarity. She could see what and how to change.

We have a client who was anxious about money, convinced he was just treading water. When we showed him how his net worth had gone from zero to six digits over the past decade, he was pleasantly surprised. The economies he'd put in place had even allowed him to buy a house. He'd done well and hadn't even realized it. Reviewing his financial plan gave him the clarity he needed to relax and continue his good habits.

To keep that clarity, you need to dust off your plan from time to time. Put an easy-to-remember date in your calendar so you won't forget. Many people consider December 31 their personal year-end. When your statements arrive in the new year, tally everything up and compare it to the year before. Are you on track? Has your net worth grown? Do you need to tweak your plan?

Step 4: Segue into savings

In previous chapters, we touched on the value of saving. Now we'd like to say it loud and clear: We consider savings a *must*.

Think of saving money as paying yourself before others. Make it a priority under the Need category of your budget. Why? <u>Savings provide an important cushion in case life takes an unforeseen turn.</u>

Are you in a similar situation? Do you have a cushion? And how much is enough? Some people set aside 10% of what they earn; others, less or more. There's no magic formula. Sitting down with a financial planner will help you determine how much you should save to meet your goals.

Whatever amount you budget for savings, have it automatically deducted from your income and directed to a savings or investment account. You won't miss what you don't see.

Don't let your excess money sit in a savings account either. Gone are the days when you could build a tidy nest egg that way. When you've saved up what you feel is a modestly comfortable amount, shift it to an investment vehicle that meets your tolerance for risk. We recommend seeking a professional's advice to do this.

We're always surprised when some clients tell us they take no satisfaction from saving, that saving does nothing for them. Don't think of it that way. Saving gives money purpose. It allows money to do something for you, or for your family and friends, your community, communities elsewhere, or a cause you care about.

You may feel that saving forces you to make do with less. We'd argue that saving gives you more. It makes you feel better-off, more in control of your spending, more confident about your future. What you save today determines how wealthy you'll be later, how much you'll have to live on when you retire, and what you'll leave to your heirs. The more money you have when you stop working, the less stress you'll have in your years of retirement.

Numbers tell the story best. For illustration purposes, let's play with some scenarios:

- 35 years ago, you started with zero and began saving $100 on the first of each month. You invested in bonds or a bond fund and earned an average of 4% per year. You've never touched the money and the interest has compounded. Today you would have over $90,000.

- 25 years ago, you began saving as above. Today you would have over $50,000.
- 15 years ago, you began saving as above. Today you would have about $25,000.
- 5 years ago, you began saving as above. Today you would have about $6,600.

As you can see, the earlier you start saving, the more you'll have later, when you need it. Now, let's up the ante.

- 35 years ago, you started with zero and began saving $200 on the first of each month. You invested and earned an average of 5% per year. You've never touched the money and the interest has compounded. Today you have $228,165.
- 25 years ago, you began saving as above. Today you have $119,598.
- 15 years ago, you began saving as above. Today you have $53,680.
- 5 years ago, you began saving as above. Today you have $13,658.

All that money came from your monthly budget. It came from your commitment to differentiating between Need and Want.

Magic? No. It's discipline. You were disciplined enough to pay yourself first, and disciplined enough not to spend what you saved.

Step 5: Build your personal financial plan

Every success story starts with a plan. A plan is like a map or a GPS, pointing you to where you want to go.

Like many of our clients, you may be surprised by your budget and your net worth. You may be wondering how those numbers fit in with your financial goals. It takes experience and skill to turn your personal balance sheet into the personal financial plan that predicts different scenarios for your financial future and helps you reach your goals.

A financial plan shows you how things will look in 5 to 30 years based on what you're doing now. Many people are living longer than their parents and grandparents did. Outliving your money is a definite concern. Building a plan now, and keeping it accurate as your situation changes, can have a huge impact on your financial success over time.

What can affect your plan's accuracy? For a start, there's inflation. Then there's the rate of return on your investments. And don't forget changes to tax laws and other legislation, changes in your family and health status, overspending, and loss of income.

Growing wealth is a complex business. Would you drill and fill your own teeth? Represent yourself in court? It takes an expert to produce an accurate financial plan, and an expert to update it as things change. A financial planner knows exactly how to turn your information into a plan that's right for you. A financial planner will provide the clarity and the confidence you'll need over the coming years.

Many financial advisors aren't financial planners. Be sure to seek someone certified in both skills, or look for two different people to help plan your future. In Chapter 6, we'll talk more about the trusted specialists you'll want on your team as you build and follow your plan.

———— ∞ ————

The first suggestions came slowly. Ellen, who'd worked at the garden centre the longest, murmured something about a better website for online ordering. Marcus said that if they used more suppliers, they could shop around for better prices, maybe try some unusual varieties.

After a few minutes, the discussion caught fire. Soon ideas were tumbling out and everyone was talking, nodding, grinning.

Should she say it? *Could* she say it?

The only thing Rose hated more than the avocado green bathroom in her Seventies Museum condo, and the spreadsheet software Laurel kept telling her to use, was public speaking. Every time there was a break in the discussion and she thought of offering her idea, her palms went slick with sweat and her tongue became a wedge of sandpaper. It makes no sense, she thought. How can one part of me be soaking and another part so dry?

Mrs. Birch looked up from her notebook, where she was writing down people's ideas, and locked eyes with Rose. "Who hasn't had a turn?"

No, thought Rose. Not me. Please.

Mrs. Birch smiled. Not her full-on glorious sunshine ray smile, but a gentler version that lifted Rose up and shook a few words out of her.

"I thought we could . . . " Wait, should she have raised her hand? She put it halfway up, realized how silly she must look, and snatched it back down. Then, like a fool, she glanced at Tripp. He looked at her, feet apart, muscled arms folded, eyes shooting bright blue beams. No one could have eyes like that. He had to wear coloured contacts. And he was probably late because he spent all morning in front of the mirror arranging his hair to look just right. For sure he was one of those vain, self-centred guys who looked at women that way, just *looked* at them, with those eyes, just to see what happened.

Mrs. Birch had followed Rose's gaze. She shot Tripp a withering look before turning back to Rose. "Please, go on. I'd love to know what you think."

Rose took a deep breath. "Master Gardeners," she blurted out. Oh no. Please, no—was that saliva? Did she just spit in front of everyone?

"Okay," said Mrs. Birch. "Tell us more."

So Rose told them, hesitantly but gradually gaining confidence, especially when Jasmine chimed in with "Awesome idea, Rosie!"

Mrs. Birch scribbled furiously. "So we'd have a Master Gardener table here, what do you think—two, three days a week?"

Rose nodded. "I'm happy to be the first volunteer. On my day off, of course. Lots of the others from my courses would be up for it. You know, having them here to answer people's questions, it's probably not going to mean big sales right away. But those customers will come back. It'll build loyalty."

"Loyalty." Mrs. Birch turned slowly to face Tripp. "Yes." Her voice went icy and she enunciated every syllable. That's something we could use more of around here, wouldn't you say, Lawrence?"

He winced as if she had struck him.

YOUR FINANCIAL JOURNAL

Keeping a financial journal is integral to your plan and your success in following it. We're big believers in "write it down, make it happen." When you record information, ideas, goals, and plans, you make them real and concrete. They're harder to ignore than if they stay vague notions in your head.

In your journal so far, you should have a copy of your budget and your net worth calculations. You may have recorded your daily and weekly expenses for a while to get an idea of what they add up to each month. You'll have answers to the questions we asked in the Five Steps to Financial Success, and you'll have a list of goals plus realistic ideas for how to achieve them.

We encourage you to add to your journal. Keep it a work in progress. It's a great place to note down anything that relates to your financial life— new goals, commitments, dreams, feelings, reminders, major expenditures. A lot of what you write will tie in to your budget, net worth, and goals. That's why we recommend keeping all this information in one place.

Here are a few more topics to consider including in your journal. For each, besides writing your general thoughts, try to note your starting point, your destination, and the action plan that will get you there.

We'll cover some of these topics, like retirement and insurance, in more detail later in this book.

Cash flow and major purchases
Anyone who earns money makes choices about how to spend it. Your cash flow—what you earn and what you spend—is affected not only by your regular budget but also by any big expenditures that come along.

What major purchases do you see emerging in your life? A home? A car? A boat? A diamond ring? A new roof? A new dishwasher? Write them down. Think hard, really hard—are they Need or Want items? Write them into your budget under the appropriate column. Now, take notes on how you will pay or save for each item. The sooner you start planning for big expenses, the easier it will be to handle them.

Building and protecting net worth
Ideally, you'll want to see your net worth grow year by year until it reaches a point where you're comfortable with it. Once you've built it up, you can start to do things with it.

What net worth are you aiming for? Write it down. Once you've spoken with a professional and come up with a solid financial plan, you'll have a better idea of what this figure should be. How can you continue to build your net worth? How can you keep it from eroding? Write down any ideas you have.

Retirement

Many people, when they think about retirement, think in numbers. At what age do you see yourself retiring? How much income do you think you'll need to fund your retirement goals? Put those numbers in your journal.

But there are other things to think about. What do you see yourself *doing* in retirement? Will you travel the world? Write it down and put a price tag on it. Will you volunteer more? Where, and how often?

Education

Do you think you'll continue your education at some point, whether to land a better job or just to have fun? Write down what you'd like to study. How much will it cost? How long will it take? Where can you take courses? Jot down your ideas for making it all happen.

What about paying for your children's higher education? Are you in favour of helping? Or do you think kids value their education more when they pay their own way? If you want to contribute, write down the role you see yourself playing. Will you pay their tuition? Their textbooks? Their room and board? Their beer and movie money?

Income tax

Does anyone ever want to pay more tax? We didn't think so. If reducing your income tax, now and in future, is one of your goals, add a note about that to your journal.

There are tax-efficient options out there. Write down the best ways of finding out what they are. Will you do some research yourself? Talk to your accountant or financial advisor? We definitely recommend getting some professional advice.

Life insurance

Your family needs to be provided for if the number 7 bus has your name on it and you die unexpectedly. What exactly do you need to insure? Cash flow to sustain a spouse or child? Outstanding debts such as a mortgage or car loan? Taxes owing on a cottage?

Write down how much income you bring in each year and whether someone other than you relies on that money. Write down the ages of your children and how long they'll be dependent on you. Note your total debts and any other amounts you're responsible for. Then talk to a qualified life insurance specialist about your options.

Disability insurance

If illness or injury knocks you flat and you're unable to work, you and your family still need to be provided for. If your injury is temporary, how will you cover the missing income? What if your condition is long-term or chronic? What will you do then?

Figure out what income would be lost if you or your spouse became disabled. Then talk to a qualified life insurance specialist about whether disability insurance is right for you.

Estate transfer and legacy planning

You'll want to make sure that after you die, your estate is transferred in the most tax-efficient way possible. Do you have specific bequests for family, friends, or charitable organizations? Or do you want to leave this world clutching your last dollar to your chest?

If you want to leave a legacy, write down how much and for whom. To make sure your wishes are followed, carry through by getting a legal will.

Business planning

If you own your own business, chances are you won't be running it forever. Whether you end up sitting on a beach in Hawaii, or living the high life in Paris, or exiting this life altogether, you'll want some kind of succession plan for your business.

Write down how you see the future of your business if you're not part of it. What should happen to the business? Do you want specific people to benefit from it? Do you want someone to take over and continue your work? How do *they* feel about that?

Lifestyle planning

Moncy is only as good as what you exchange it for. Having a happy, productive life means understanding what matters to you. Then you can exchange your money for the things and experiences that enrich your life and the lives of those you care for.

Do you love to travel? Does volunteering overseas inspire you? Have you always wanted to learn a new skill, maybe acting or the violin or martial arts? Do you dream of painting watercolours in the desert? Spending summers by a lake? Only you know what kind of lifestyle appeals to you. Keep writing your ideas in your journal, and keep figuring out how to make them happen.

Rose was on cash, counting down the hour until she could be out back tending to plants instead of customers, when Mrs. Birch appeared.

"Great idea yesterday, Rose. I can't wait for our Master Gardener service to start up."

"Oh. Thank you." Rose ducked her head. She still felt shy around the new owner, who this cool morning was wearing a cream fisherman-knit sweater with a peacock-hued pashmina draped over one shoulder. Topaz earrings dangled against her long silver-white hair. Garden chic, thought Rose, looking down at her standard-issue polo shirt. Another perk of being the owner.

"You know, people think a successful business is all about the numbers." Mrs. Birth flicked a smidgen of soil off the counter. "That's not really true. It's about ideas. Think big, brainstorm a bunch of ideas, keep the best ones, make them happen. That's really all there is to it."

"But the numbers matter," came a voice from behind them. "If they didn't, I'd be out of a job." Laurel set her purse on the counter and gave her mother a tight grin.

"Sweetie! What a nice surprise."

"Hi, Mom." They hugged quickly over the counter.

"This is my daughter, Laurel," said Rose. "Laurel, this is Mrs. Birch, the new owner I was telling you about."

Mrs. Birch took Laurel's hand, covered it briefly with her other one. "A numbers woman, are you?"

"Guilty as charged. I'm an accountant."

"How wonderful." Mrs. Birch smiled. "You're right, of course. But believe me, numbers are no good unless they've got ideas behind them. Your mother here is an ideas woman."

"Don't I know it," Laurel said.

Just then Tripp walked by, balancing an armload of empty planters. Once again Rose stared, her eyes reminding her that they were the boss of her and would look wherever they pleased, thank you very much.

Only when Tripp disappeared around the corner did Rose become aware of Mrs. Birch's long-fingered hand on her arm. "Take it from me," the woman said quietly. "Not all ideas are good ones. Some are truly terrible."

Rose's cheeks flamed. What does she have against the guy? Why is she always so cold toward him? She eyed the age spots on Mrs. Birch's elegant wrinkled hand. This woman had been around awhile, might be old enough to be Rose's mother, and succeeded at everything she did. Whatever she knew about Tripp, if it was serious enough to warn Rose off, it was probably worth paying attention to.

Rose looked at Mrs. Birch and, her heart sinking, nodded.

6

Your Helpers

As the new owner glided off—she was so tall and poised . . . had she been a runway model? a ballet dancer?—all the energy that had animated Laurel's mother when Laurel walked into the store drained away.

"What brings you in, sweetie?" Rose's voice sounded flat and tired. "You look pretty, by the way."

"Oh, Mom." Laurel patted the green and blue silk scarf she'd looped around her neck in a desperate attempt at cheerfulness. Two days had passed, yet she still hadn't cast off the pall of her last-ever date. "You know Reena, our office manager? It's her birthday. I need a big bouquet, something gorgeous, exotic."

"I'm on cash for another hour, but let me call Jasmine. She's great at arrangements. You coming back for it later? We could do lunch—"

Laurel glanced at her watch. "No, I have to take it now. I've got two meetings this morning, a conference call at noon, another meeting after that." She swallowed. "I'm so behind."

While her mother called Jasmine on the portable radio, Laurel surveyed the unblocked aisles, the neat shelves of garden tools, and the display of seeds that for once featured no packets jutting out at odd angles.

Only three days under new ownership and already the place was shipshape. "Everything in its place," she murmured.

"And a place for everything."

Laurel turned. A short, stocky man smiled widely, turning a hat around in his hands. "Ben Franklin, right?" A soft British accent coloured his clear voice.

Laurel shrugged. "I have no idea."

"Well, it's an apt expression." His cheeks shone like polished apples, and he continued to beam at her, rocking on his heels. Laurel glanced at his feet, took in the thick-soled walking shoes made of dull black leather. Nerd shoes. What possessed anyone to buy such things and then actually wear them? In public?

"Allan Greenspan." The man stuck out a hand. Good manners and the presence of her mother urged Laurel to take it.

"Really," she said, pumping his hand, "I have no idea where it comes from. It's just something my father likes to say. Though it sounds like an old quote. I doubt it was Greenspan."

"No, me." He laughed from deep in his belly. "I mean, I'm Allan Greenspan."

She peered at him. Was this some kind of joke? This guy was seriously weird.

"I know." He set his hat on the counter next to Laurel's purse. A fedora? Is that what it was called? The men wore them in all those black-and-white films that Mom watched. "It's my curse in life," he was saying. "Being named after a famous economist. All the worse because A, he's still alive and kicking, and B, I don't know the first thing about economics."

"Honey, Jasmine will be here in a second." Rose stashed the radio beneath the counter. "She knows you're in a hurry."

The man's face fell. "Oh, so you're rushing off, then?"

"Mm-hmm." Laurel saw Jasmine outside, wiping her hands on her tattered jeans. "Look, Mom, I'll go with her, give her some idea of what Reena likes. Call you tonight, okay?"

As Laurel headed for the door, she didn't look back. She didn't need to. She could feel them on her, the quirky man's eyes, the whole time.

Do you believe that success depends on luck? As you can probably tell from what you've read so far, we believe you make your own luck. When it comes to money, having goals, a financial plan, and a well-balanced mix of diversified investments that you shape and prune as needed goes a long way toward increasing your good luck and minimizing your bad luck.

A balanced, diversified portfolio that's matched to your goals, age, and risk tolerance involves a lot less "strike it lucky" and a lot more "steady as she goes." You may not find "steady as she goes" very exciting, but history has repeatedly shown that it works.

Professionals aren't bored with the "steady as she goes" approach. They rely on it. They know that a long, steady growing season is one of the best conditions for a financial garden.

This chapter is about choosing the team who will help you grow your money. When it comes to expert jobs, we tend to rely on experts—mechanics, tailors, cabinetmakers, surgeons, real estate agents, systems analysts, even pet groomers. Why would managing the money you need to see you through your life be any different? The knowledgeable, trustworthy members you pick for your team will guide you through all kinds of important money management decisions.

Maybe you prefer to do it yourself (DIY). Maybe you've read up on investments, or your Uncle Bill has done well with his Internet stock-picking system and is willing to share his tips. That's great. We'll talk more about the DIY approach in this chapter. Going it alone may seem appealing, but it has some downsides.

Growing your financial garden, and avoiding large and costly mistakes along the way, takes a team of experienced professionals you can trust. You're an important part of that team, but it should have other members, like a banker, lawyer, accountant, financial advisor and/or financial planner. It's also great if your team has supporters on the sidelines—family and friends who have solid life experience, know something about finances, and have your best interests at heart.

CHOOSING YOUR TEAM MEMBERS

Banker

Your banker will help you manage your accounts and handle transactions like converting money, increasing or paying down your line of credit, and applying for a credit card. More and more, much banking happens online but a relationship with a real person has benefits. Your banker can be a good resource to you.

Mortgage Broker

A mortgage broker will help with mortgage approvals, interest rate guidance, and other mortgage details. They will review your personal situation and recommend best alternatives for you.

Lawyer

Sooner or later you will need a lawyer, whether you're buying your first home, getting a divorce, drawing up or probating a will, or getting yourself or a loved one out of trouble. Choose a lawyer who specializes in the practice that meets your specific need. Experience matters, so keep that in mind.

Ask how you'll be billed for your lawyer's services and request an estimate at your first meeting. Come to meetings prepared. You'll save money if you keep your questions and discussions brief and on point.

Accountant

We encourage you to hire an accountant to help with your taxes and tax planning. An accountant will help you make smart financial decisions from a tax perspective.

When choosing an accountant, you may want to ask about years of experience, fees, specialties, and knowledge and experience relevant to your situation. Can you call the accountant if you have more questions? You need an accountant who communicates clearly and makes time for you.

Financial advisor/financial planner

Financial advisor is a broad term used by many professionals who help people manage money. A financial advisor will, for instance, manage your investment portfolio and retirement fund, aiming for returns that meet your goals and your comfort with risk. A financial planner specializes in planning to meet long-term goals. A financial planner will review your overall financial landscape, help you create a personal plan, and monitor and adjust that plan over time.

Many financial planners are also financial advisors, but not all financial advisors are licensed financial planners. Be sure you understand the services you need, and make sure the person—or people—you choose are able and qualified to provide those services.

Ask which specific services you're paying for, how much those services cost, and how the advisor/planner will be paid. Fees vary. Don't be embarrassed to ask for these details. Professionals are required to explain how they get compensated.

Choose wisely

Not all bankers, lawyers, accountants, financial advisors, and financial planners are created, or educated, equally. Backgrounds and educational credentials vary widely, even within specific disciplines.

When you see initials or credentials you don't understand, ask what they mean. It never hurts to contact the credential-issuing institution to confirm that the person you're interested in earned the credentials there and remains a member in good standing. The quality of the firm you work with matters and a good one holds its staff to high standards.

It may also be a good idea to get a referral from a trusted family member, friend, or co-worker.

Once you've assembled it, your team of wisely chosen professionals can lead you down the right financial path. Every path has its stones— markets rise and fall, interest rates fluctuate, tax laws change—but a steady strategy, solid goals, and a supportive team will produce positive results over time.

"I'd like something shade-loving, please. Tried my own hand at picking and sadly, it went badly wrong." The compact man rocked slightly as he spoke. "Fairly tidy. It's a small corner, no room to spread. Found that out the hard way. "

He must be a monk, Rose decided. He sported a monk's tonsure, anyway, the top of his head smooth and shiny under the fluorescent lights. He beamed at her. At least he was a merry monk. "Annual or perennial?" she asked.

"Oh, annual. You never know what next year will bring."

Did he just wink at her? Rose shook her head slightly, hoping to clear the cobwebs that had spun across her mind after Mrs. Birch's warning.

The man leaned in close; she could smell his pepperminty breath. "Tell me now and tell me straight, as they say in the films. Your daughter is delightful and there is no wedding ring in sight. What are my chances?"

Rose inhaled sharply. Not a monk, then.

"Please, please. No need to spare my feelings. I'd rather know now and get it over with immediately."

"Get what over with?"

"Well, life, of course." The man snatched his hat—a fedora, Rose noticed, surprised and despite herself a little impressed—and clutched it to his heart in mock agony. "If I can't see her again, there's no point, really. To perennials or annuals, to poetry or beauty, to any of it."

DOING IT YOURSELF

We know that the "do it yourself" approach is important to some people. Some, by nature, prefer to go it alone. Some think they'll do as well as, or even better than, a professional if they manage their money themselves. Others have a real interest in money and want to learn by doing. And still others are keen to save on commissions and fees.

Armed with self-insight, knowledge, and the latest software, some people manage and grow their money quite successfully. Many don't.

We urge you to think about the consequences of DIY. If you mess up investments that are earmarked for your retirement, you could be in serious trouble in the years ahead. If your portfolio is full of low- to no-risk investments, your money may not be growing enough to keep up with inflation, and it may not be enough to live on when you need it. If you rely on high-risk investments, you may face major losses if the market shifts.

Don't close your mind to your options. Hiring a professional doesn't mean handing over full control of your life. Professionals give advice— you're still the one who signs on the dotted line. And using a pro may be a better value than you think, especially when you consider that investment mistakes can cost you dearly, if not now, then in the future. There's plenty of excellent help out there. Ask around and you'll find it.

Before you opt for DIY, we'd like to wave a few red flags. Unless you're experienced and comfortable with *all* these areas, don't try to go it alone.

Red Flag 1: Will time tell?

Investing money well takes energy and time. Doing it right is a full-time job (and then some) for professionals in the field. And the pros rely on others to help them, receiving as-it-happens input from a battery of domestic and international specialists. If you try to do all of this on your own, it's the equivalent of several full-time jobs, plus overtime.

Do you have the time to manage your money properly? And how will you find all the information you need? How will you even *know* what you need to find out?

Red Flag 2: Will your DIY desire last?

To manage your finances well, you have to really want to take it on. A lot of investment information—economic commentaries, analysts' research reports, and so on—is tinder-dry. Do you want to plough through it all week after week, year after year?

Red Flag 3: How reliable are your sources?

How will you know if what you read and hear is credible? Just because something's written on paper, posted on the Internet, or whispered as a hot tip doesn't make it true.

Where do you get your ideas? What's the track record of the person, publication, or website in which you've placed your faith (not to mention, potentially, your finances)? Are you following a reliable investment strategy?

Red Flag 4: What's in your portfolio and plan?

Financial professionals know that a sound portfolio needs balance and diversity. It needs a mix of assets matched to your individual situation. What's more, your portfolio needs to mesh with your larger financial goals and your plan for the future. Keeping all those balls in the air takes some skillful juggling.

Who's going to monitor your portfolio to make sure your balanced asset weightings don't get out of whack? Who's going to suggest you take some profit to reduce a holding that has doubled? Who's going to put you on a personal savings plan to make sure your retirement fund grows as projected? Are you willing to do all these things yourself?

Red Flag 5: Who's watching your back?

Buying stocks, bonds, and mutual funds is one thing, but who will fine-tune your financial plan when life deals you a surprise? Who's your sounding board for financial ideas? Are your friends and family the most knowledgeable people to comment on what you're doing? Do they really understand money, and do they always have the bigger picture in mind?

Say you're sorely tempted by a shiny new sports car. You really want it, your spouse really wants it, your friends think you deserve it. Having someone on your team to check with before you stray from your plan may make you think twice. If buying the car means postponing retirement for two years, is it really worth it? Managing your emotions is one of the most important and difficult parts of investing and financial planning. Having a trusted but impartial person watching your back can help.

Red Flag 6: How will you stay current?

All the professionals we've suggested for your team are trained for what they do. But their education doesn't stop with their credentials. Financial advisors and planners, for instance, continually upgrade their education as part of their licensing. Ongoing training is a must in an industry where the climate and regulations are always changing.

If you deal with a professional, you'll get up-to-date advice based on current conditions and laws. If your team member works at a large, respected firm, you can be sure a compliance department or supervisory manager will be monitoring their work on your behalf. If you go it alone, how will you stay current? Unless you know how the industry and markets are changing and what the regulations demand, you may be in for some costly mistakes.

"You know that guy or something?" Jasmine asked. "The one talking to your mom?"

Laurel shook her head. She stood straight and faced the glass display case, its shelves alive with fresh-cut flowers of all hues. No way was she turning around and risking eye contact with the strange little British man.

Jasmine added two sprays of freesia to the bouquet. "For the smell," she said. "Colour's one thing, but you need a little perfume too. Seriously, he keeps staring at you."

"I have no idea who he is."

"Makes me think of your mom. When that new guy walks by, she forgets what she's saying, she forgets everything. Her eyes bug out and all she can do is gawk at him. Just like that guy's gawking at you."

"My mom?"

"Yeah, with that new guy, Tripp. He started a few days ago, when Mrs. Birch took over. *She* doesn't like him, that's for sure, but your mom, she's got it bad."

"My *mom*?"

Jasmine paused, a giant fern in one hand. "What's wrong here? I'm pretty sure I'm speaking English. In fact, I'm a hundred percent sure. It's the only language I know."

"I just—" Laurel tried to let the idea sink in. "My mom is not the type to gawk at anyone. Especially a man. Not since my dad . . .".

Jasmine fanned out the fern at the back of the bouquet. "So what happened with her and your dad anyway? I mean, your mom and me are pretty tight. I tell her about my love life sometimes." The girl flushed. Still so young, Laurel thought. "But she won't talk about the divorce."

Laurel sighed. Her mother had always been private, but on this topic her lips were buttoned. Laurel herself didn't exactly know what prompted the split. Her parents had been married forever, they never fought, seldom even disagreed. Mind you, they never talked much either, but they seemed to like it that way. That, Laurel never understood. She needed words, lots of them. It was how Matthew had stolen her heart. They'd gone on for hours when they first met, stayed up whole nights telling stories and confiding dreams. Now, her life without him rang silent.

Silence had always featured large in her parents' marriage. Laurel's dad was a talker, like her, but just not with her mom. Counselling might have done them some good. When the subject of divorce came up, Laurel was surprised. "We both love you, honey" was all he'd say the few times she probed. "This has nothing to do with our feelings for you."

"Mom won't talk to me either," Laurel told Jasmine. "Everyone was in shock when they split up, me included. All I know is that Dad didn't leave her for anyone. He lives alone. He has ever since he moved to the east coast. So if you find anything out, clue me in, okay?"

WORKING WITH A FINANCIAL ADVISOR

Your advisor, whether a banker, an investment advisor, or a financial planner, is a key member of your team. A good advisor is someone who puts your best interests first in what should be a long-term relationship.

That may mean delivering tough news, like "You're not saving enough" or "No, I won't do that for you; it's not the right thing." Or it may mean saying, "Spend a little more. You're accumulating more than you need. What about an extra gift for the kids at Christmas, or doing something meaningful for a charity?"

There's nothing more satisfying for a financial advisor than to watch the seeds you and your team planted flourish over the years.

Be honest

As we've said before, a financial plan is a powerful tool for putting you on the right path and showing you whether you're still on it. Your plan will tell you, based on your current savings and spending, whether you're going to reach your financial, charitable, educational, and life goals. Inaccurate or incomplete data will produce a useless plan.

That's why you must be honest with yourself and your financial advisor as you draft your financial plan. You need to provide straight-up information. If your details aren't correct, the output will be inaccurate and the projections and plan of action will be useless.

Your advisor will ask you a lot of questions, including some you may not have thought about. They aren't meant to intrude on your privacy. We understand that stripping yourself bare of your financial secrets can feel like an invasion of privacy. We know it can be embarrassing to talk to someone you hardly know about your monthly spending. But if you're serious about improving your financial position, you have to answer questions honestly so your advisor can prepare a realistic plan for your future.

Know your priorities

You also need to be clear about what you want in life. It's okay if you don't want to leave money to the kids or to charity. It's okay if you don't think you need to save because you're expecting a large inheritance. It's okay if you really need to spend $400 a month on piano lessons or lunch with friends.

These are highly personal choices about what's important to you. All you need to do is be up-front about them. Your advisor needs to know as much as possible about your true priorities, goals, and cash flow in order to make accurate projections in your financial plan.

We heard a story recently about a couple in their mid-40s. Both worked; together they netted $150,000 a year. They spent every cent, setting aside nothing for savings or retirement. They felt that all the things they bought were Need items. Realizing they weren't making financial headway, they asked a financial advisor how to save some money each month so they could eventually buy a house and retire in ten years.

The advisor they consulted noted that they leased expensive cars, rented a spacious and expensive view apartment, ate out almost every day, and spent large sums on clothing, jewellery, and accessories. They understood that they earned more than many people, but they'd never paid attention to where their money went.

It soon became clear that this couple lived well beyond their means, and the only way they were going to save any money was to change their spending habits. They listened politely to the advisor's simple suggestions: rent a less expensive apartment, lease less expensive cars once the present leases expire, eat at home more often, buy fewer and less expensive clothes and accessories.

The advisor told them that differentiating between Need and Want was an important step toward their goal of building a down payment and saving for retirement. The advisor explained that no matter who you are or what you earn, if you don't live within your means, you can't save money. The advisor also explained that it's not what you earn but what you *save*, and what you do with those savings, that creates wealth. If you spend all your money and don't invest in a home or your retirement (if those are your goals), time will soon pass and you likely won't retire when and how you want.

In the end, to the advisor's surprise, the couple decided to disregard the advice and continue their current lifestyle because they were unwilling to give up the luxuries they enjoyed.

Everyone has different priorities, and actions speak louder than words. If owning a home and having a comfortable retirement are your most important goals, you'll be more likely to do what you have to do to make those goals a reality. If you'd rather enjoy life now and worry about the future later, that's your personal choice. No advisor can or will override your decision.

Share your experiences

Your advisor needs to know something about your experiences, where you're coming from and why, to understand your attitude toward investing.

Here's a story we've heard similar versions of from clients. When they grew up, Dad looked after the finances and Mom looked after the home. Even if Mom worked, Dad typically handled the investing. Dad didn't do well. In extreme cases, the family had to move out of their home because Dad lost the equity on some gold mining company that was a sure thing.

If you grew up in that sort of environment, it's no surprise that as an adult you'd have an aversion to investing. Children don't know the difference between gambling on penny stocks and investing in quality corporations. Childhood experiences like these often make people very conservative when it comes to their investment portfolio.

Other clients tell us their parents scrimped hard to pay the mortgage and balance the budget. That sort of childhood experience can also lead people to be cautious about risking any of their hard-earned money.

We also hear about the investment mistakes clients have made themselves. These stories often involve hot tips about investment schemes. With no one as a sounding board except the people suggesting the investments, of course the tips sound great. But because such investments are risky, they often fail.

When you make a poor investment and lose all or most of your money, the experience may sour you on further investments. Don't let that happen. Steer clear of hot tips and shady schemes. If you get tempting advice from trusted friends or family, don't shut them out, but *do* consult a professional.

If any of these stories sound familiar, don't feel embarrassed. They're common. When you share your experiences, it helps your advisor to understand your comfort level with investment and to tailor a plan to your needs. It's no good saying you want big returns, are fine owning stocks, and can handle the volatility if you honestly can't. Besides talking to you about this, your advisor may ask you to complete a questionnaire to determine how comfortable you are with risk.

Build your knowledge

How knowledgeable are you about finances? Do you know a lot, a little, or zilch? You need to be up-front about your level of knowledge so your advisor can educate you and explain what's what as you work together.

Learning more about finances and the stock market will make a difference to how you feel about discussing your needs and wants. It's natural to fear what you don't know or understand. When you understand the difference between gambling on a penny stock and investing in a solid, tangible business, you'll be better equipped to make sound decisions about your money. When you know that a business you're investing in employs thousands of people and generates billions of dollars a year—including a quarterly profit dividend to you—you'll be more comfortable and confident about that investment.

Still, no matter how much you know, markets and share prices don't always act reasonably or rationally. The investment world can at times feel daunting, confusing, complex, and frustrating.

That's when you need to trust your team. Your advisor may offer suggestions that are beyond your comfort zone, but don't let that stop you. Sometimes an advisor's *job* is to make you feel uncomfortable. If you aren't at all risk-averse, your advisor may need to rein you in. If you're too timid, your advisor may have to explain why you need more growth in your portfolio.

How can you get more knowledgeable? Take courses in personal finance. Read unbiased, credible books. Ask your team members questions about anything that's unfamiliar. Building a basic level of understanding will give you some control over your finances, as well as a fighting chance of knowing whether what someone else says or recommends is reasonable.

———⚬⚬⚬———

As the old saying goes, the right time to invest is when you have money. If you've assembled a team you can rely on, and you feel you're getting good advice, you can comfortably invest money whenever you have it.

That sense of comfort is one of the biggest advantages of having trusted advisors by your side. So is the assurance of knowing that your plan includes a balanced mix of investments, tailored to your personal level of risk, which we'll discuss in the next chapter.

———⚬⚬⚬———

The cheerful British man lingered at the front cash, regaling Rose with stories in between customers and stealing more than the occasional glance at Laurel, until she finally edged out, face hidden behind an immense bouquet. Before Rose knew it, Ellen appeared to replace her on cash.

"We've been talking for over half an hour," Rose marvelled. The time had sped by in the company of this jovial man, who Rose had learned was new to town, taught history at the nearby college, loved to cook—anything with cheese in it, he told her—and was already hailed by the regulars at the Darbyshire, the busy downtown pub. He'd never been married, he offered, though he was engaged briefly. She had disappeared with another man, so suddenly she forgot to return the diamond. That was what prompted him to leave England.

"I know so much about you," Rose told the man, "but I don't know your name."

"Allan Greenspan, at your service." He snapped off a two-fingered salute. "Most people call me Al. Though it's clear you are not most people."

She rolled her eyes. "Save your flattery. If you're hoping to get anywhere with my daughter, it will have to be on your own charms. I'm not playing cupid."

"What about gardener? Would you play gardener? I'd pay you, of course."

The front door whooshed open and, from the corner of her eye, she saw him stride in. Always in motion, this Tripp.

"It's not big," Al was saying. "It's a tiny house, really, garden the size of a handkerchief, but every inch is either bare soil or a desperate tangle. I don't know where to begin. I've never had a garden, you see. Never grown a thing except for potted basil and a gigantic crush on your daughter."

"I'm not the best person to build your garden," said Rose. As Tripp came nearer, she summoned up every ounce of courage. "But I know who is."

7

Your Plants

Rose's safety shoes were ugly—thick, scuffed, tightly laced, decidedly unfeminine. Ugly. Why doesn't anyone design beautiful safety shoes for women, she wondered. She had never so intently scrutinized the footwear her job obliged her to wear, but now that she'd finally managed to speak to Tripp, it was the only place she could look.

"I might have a client for you."

"Okay."

"He's right there." She looked across the store at Al, who grinned, nodded and bounced, all at the same time.

"Okay."

"He's British." Why in the heck did she say that? As if it mattered. Her gift for spouting nonsense during the most basic of interactions astounded her.

"That's fine." Tripp started toward Al, then stopped. "Thank you, Rose." He smiled faintly then walked to greet Al.

It was the longest conversation they'd had, a word, maybe two, more than when he'd introduced himself at the staff meeting. It was the first time he ever said her name. It was enough. Rose was in love.

———— ∞ ————

When setting out your garden, you can't plant just anything in just any place. Hostas need shade; lilacs need sun. Hydrangeas prefer well-drained soil; astilbes like it wet. To make your plants bloom, you first need to know your garden's conditions and spend time preparing the land. Only then can you choose the right mix of plants that will thrive and look beautiful together.

In Part One of this book, you spent time getting prepared, getting to know who you are, where you are, and where you want to go. You prepared by thinking about your financial plan and the team who will help you with it. Now you're ready to plant the seeds of your investments.

As with growing a garden, growing wealth involves using instruments and techniques that may be new to you. In this chapter, we'll introduce some of them. Because doing things you've never done before may feel risky, this chapter also talks about risk— how comfortable you are with it and how you can learn to take and manage it.

———— ∞ ————

TYPES OF INVESTMENTS

Term deposits and GICs, bonds, stocks, and mutual funds are some of the many different types of investments out there. We'll briefly explain what each type is and how it works before discussing strategies for growing your portfolio by reducing risk.

Term deposits and GICs

If you ask your banker to put your money in something that will earn interest but that's safe, chances are it will be a term deposit or a GIC (guaranteed investment certificate). With these instruments, your money is invested, and often locked in, for a set period of time. Over that time, you build up a specified amount of interest until your investment matures.

Your term deposit or GIC is backed by the quality of the bank or institution where you buy it. If you deal with a reputable bank or firm, you can be confident that your money will be returned with interest. Also, ask if your money is insured by CDIC (Canada Deposit Insurance Corporation). This means the Government of Canada will insure your deposit up to $100,000.

Bonds

A bond is a fixed-income security offered by governments and companies. You can lend them money for a set time period and at a fixed interest rate. A bond normally pays back your money plus the interest at the end of the lending period, the maturity date. Most also pay you interest every six months. Bonds and other fixed-income securities have a range of interest rates and risk levels. Many investors use an investment advisor to help them decide which bonds to buy and when to sell.

Stocks/Equities

An "equity" is a direct investment in a business, synonymous with a stock or share. Investment advisors often help investors in choosing which stocks to buy based on their risk tolerance, investment objectives and other factors. You can make money on a stock if the stock itself increases in value or if the company pays a dividend to those who own shares. However, the stock price can also go down and the company may not pay a dividend. A stock's value depends on many factors from the size of the company to its profitability and financial stability and the economic environment.

Mutual funds

A mutual fund is a pool of investments. It allows you to diversify by holding a portion of many more investments than you could normally purchase on your own. A professional fund manager, on your behalf, decides where to invest the money and when to buy and sell investments for the mutual fund.

Investors hold units of mutual funds. The price of your units will go up if the investments in the fund do well. If they are not doing well, the unit price falls.

⊶⊷

Laurel tucked the yellow folder inside the drawer marked A–D. Her last file today. As always, a deep feeling of satisfaction stole over her as she crossed the last item off her daily list. She didn't always make it, sometimes had to carry over a task (or two, or five) to the next morning. Those days brought no satisfaction, only guilt, followed by a thorough analysis of how and where she had wasted time during the day.

Time-wasters had certainly plagued her today. The morning stop at the garden centre, though the detour had delighted Reena, who still glowed when she left work at four-thirty, arms filled with flowers. Two texts from Greg, asking if she'd gotten his phone call and email, which cost her ten minutes and an extra latte while she fretted over whether she'd made a mistake writing him off. The call from school about the impromptu soccer game and the hurried arrangements to find someone whose house the boys could go to afterward.

Yet despite the distractions, she'd powered through her list. Gazing out her tall office window, she allowed herself one minute to feel good.

Diligent daughter, disciplined student, tireless worker. Her whole life she'd been praised for her achievements and her stamina. She grew up confident she could shoulder any project, bear any burden. Until a sports car screamed through a red light and slammed her future to the ground. Nothing she'd accomplished, not one bit of it, had tested her like the three years since Matthew died.

Year one was a write-off. She couldn't brush her hair let alone care for the twins, so her parents took over primary care for them. She couldn't eat, couldn't work. She spent half the year in bed, suffocating under blankets of grief and hopelessness and bone-deep fatigue; and half in court, ravaged by fury and raging for justice. Only when she'd seen Matthew's lawyered-up killer convicted and sentenced, if you called that cuff on the cheek sentencing, could she begin to reclaim her boys and her career.

When that happened, when she finally stuck her foot back into real life, what was waiting for her? Debt. A giant wall of it. Legal fees, therapy bills, more legal fees, the mortgage in arrears, property tax owing, household expenses, yet more legal fees—the expenses kept mounting while she kept not working. Matthew's life insurance ran out faster than she could have imagined. They'd thought they were so smart, taking out a small policy to keep their monthly payments low.

No one—not her mother, not her father, not her boss who held her job for her that long lost year—knew how much trouble Laurel was in when she resurfaced, looking like her old self: diligent, disciplined, tireless. No one knew about the new layers beneath that facade: terrified, lonely, exhausted.

MANAGING RISK

The investments described in this chapter all carry different levels of risk. Term deposits, GICs, and bonds are on the safer end of the spectrum. Stocks are on the riskier end. Mutual funds carry different levels of risk depending on the kinds of investments held within a particular fund.

Risk is a big issue for investors. When you think about risk, you may tend to focus on the chance of a big stock market drop. But you need to be aware of other risks as well. Inflation and taxes, for example, affect the long-term risk of outliving your money. Those risks are every bit as important as how your stock portfolio is invested.

Understanding and managing risk is a big part of investing

The best way to avoid making mistakes is to stick to a balanced, diversified plan that matches your tolerance for risk. A plan that's tailored to your risk level should make you feel comfortable. You may need to be flexible and change your course along the way—we're all human, and circumstances change—but you'll be better off in the long run if you have a plan to guide you.

In the sections that follow, we discuss risk in more detail. We also talk about the importance of diversifying and explain what a balanced, diversified plan might look like. Our goal is to give you strategies for investing successfully and managing your portfolio in a way that allows you to sleep at night.

Reduce risk by diversifying

The wise gardener chooses a balanced mix of plants, a strategy known as *diversification*. In investing as in gardening, diversification lowers risk. If you seek a diversified mix of investments, you'll lower the chance of a single bad investment crippling your portfolio and your financial health to the point where you can't recover.

You can diversify your investments in various ways: by the number of investments you own, by asset class, by market sector, and by geography.

Diversify the number of investments you own. Let's say you have only four stocks in your portfolio. If one of them falls by 50%, the value of your overall portfolio will drop 12.5%. That's because, all else being equal, each stock has a 25% weighting. The lesson? Because each stock has an enormous impact on your portfolio, your risk is high. Now let's say you own 15 or 20 stocks. Each stock represents just 5% to a little under 7% of your overall portfolio. Should one stock fall drastically, your portfolio won't nosedive. By owning more stocks, you've spread out your risk.

Diversify by asset class. Some examples of asset classes are cash, stocks, bonds, real estate, precious metals, art, collectibles, and commodities. Holding various types of assets reduces your risk if one should falter. When one class fares badly, another may gain ground. The stock market may languish while real estate surges ahead. Or real estate could drop while precious metals hold their own.

Diversify by market sector. If you invest in different sectors of the economy, you'll be sure to own some of what's doing well without holding too much of what's doing poorly. When the US banks suffered in 2008, for instance, that market sector took a beating. You can imagine the impact on any portfolio heavily invested in banks. Being exposed to each sector is very important. When the stock market index rises, say, 10% over a year, that performance is often attributable to just one or two market sectors. One year, technology stocks may outperform all others. Another year, health care companies may be the flavour *du jour.*

Diversify geographically. North American stock markets give you thousands of investment choices, including many of the world's biggest and best companies, but why limit yourself? Emerging economies and some developing nations have demonstrated strong growth relative to Western economies. Developing nations are also more open to investment than ever. By spreading out your investments geographically, you'll reduce the risk you may face in any one market.

Reduce the risk of inflation

Inflation affects the general cost of goods and services and investments over time. Think about the price of cars thirty years ago. Now think about salaries. Prices rise over time—it's a fact of life—but if salaries didn't rise too, we wouldn't be able to afford anything. Over time, inflation decreases the purchasing power of money.

Some pension plans are indexed to inflation. That means they gradually pay more as time goes on, generally 2% to 3% more per year, depending on the annual inflation rate. That increase allows pensioners to live at the same level year after year. If that concept makes sense to you, it will also make sense that you should invest your retirement savings so that they grow over time, just as inflation does.

Yet many people, afraid of risking their hard-earned money in the stock market, simply save it in term deposits, assuming it will lie in wait for their retirement. It will lie in wait, all right, but it likely won't have grown as much as the rate of inflation, thanks to income tax and low interest rates. Over time, the purchasing power of all that saved money will decline, with the same impact on your portfolio as if you'd lost it.

Imagine if government and corporate pension plans invested strictly in term deposits or bonds. *They'd run out of money.* Pension plans invest in a combination of stocks, bonds, and real estate. They need to grow their assets to pay retirees.

As we've said before, it's not what you make but what you save and what you *do* with those savings that creates wealth. Keeping some money in safe savings as an emergency fund makes sense in the short term. But your long-term investment or retirement portfolio should contain good-quality equities, businesses that will be around a long time and pay a dividend. That's how you can fight inflation. That's how you can end up with more money and more purchasing power in retirement, when you no longer earn a salary.

Reduce the risk of taxation
Just like inflation, taxes can eat away at your savings, leaving you with a lot less than you started with.

Paying tax on money you earn is a fact of life, one that will likely never change. Tax issues are complex and vary greatly from one jurisdiction to the next. No matter where you live or how much you earn, it's worth your while to be smart about how you earn your money. Not all income is taxed the same way.

Employment. Apart from certain deductions you're allowed to claim, you'll be taxed on all of your employment income. Because income from working is the most common way to make money, it's no surprise that it's taxed at the highest rate.

Interest. The interest you earn from a term deposit, GIC, or bond is taxed the same way as employment income. You pay tax at your *marginal tax rate*, which is based on your income. The higher your income, the higher marginal tax rate you pay. Because interest is often paid at a low rate and taxed at a high rate, earning interest isn't a very tax-efficient way of growing your assets. You're usually not left with much money after tax—often not enough to fight inflation.

Dividends. Good-quality companies pay their shareholders dividends. In Canada, dividends are taxed at a lower rate than employment income, leaving more money in your pocket. If you're comfortable investing your money in good-quality businesses over time, and you're not bothered by share-price fluctuations, you can do very well by collecting dividends.

Capital gains. You realize (receive) a capital gain any time you sell an investment for more than you paid for it. Capital gains are taxed at half the rate of earned or interest income, making them the most tax-efficient type of income. Capital gains can be earned investing, as examples, in the stock market, art, real estate (normally, excluding your personal residence), collectibles and any other good that can go up in value.

What about volatility? Individual stock and real estate prices do fluctuate, but the market goes up over time. One speaker we've heard likens investing in the stock market to going up a moving escalator while playing with a yo-yo. The yo-yo is a good, solid stock: it goes up and down, up and down, in constant motion while slowly being carried up the escalator. The escalator, of course, is the stock market. If you're patient and remain on the up escalator, you'll gradually reach the top with even more in your pocket. The same can be said of some other investments, too.

Reduce the risk of outliving your money

Many people are afraid of outliving their money. It's a valid concern. When you stop working, chances are you'll have to rely largely on the money you've saved.

If you're lucky, you may also rely on a government- or company-funded pension plan. Typically, either you will have paid into a company pension plan, your employer will have paid into it, or both of you will have paid into it. It's also typical for a pension manager to invest this money on your behalf.

Many of today's younger workers and casual employees have no employer pension to look forward to. If you're in that position, you need to start saving early so that you'll have enough income to support yourself in retirement.

Will you outlive your money? Once you stop working, what you receive from private and government pensions, and from your own invested savings, is generally a fixed amount. The key is what you spend.

If you spend more than what comes in, you'll erode your capital and go backwards, putting yourself in danger of living longer than your money. If you live within your means and spend up to the amount that comes in each month, you should be in good shape. The only way to know for sure is to record your income and spending honestly and to review your financial plan every year.

Laurel had just zipped her laptop case around her computer and four files she would preview tonight after the boys went to bed, when the office phone rang.

No name on the display, an unfamiliar number. A client? It was six-thirty, too late for most of her corporate accounts to check in. Greg? He'd already left as many messages as a man could and still hang on to his dignity.

Should she? The boys were at their friend Rodney's, waiting to be picked up. It was already past their dinner time.

Her hand hovered over the phone. Don't do it, said a voice. It could be important, said another, a new client. She decided to risk it.

"Laurel?" It was a man. Not Greg. More cheerful, boisterous. Memory nibbled at her. *British*.

By the time she had pegged the strange rocking, hatted man from the garden centre, it was too late. He'd already launched into an explanation. "Your mother loves you," he was saying, "and she's suspicious of me. Rightly so. I'm a suspicious character, always have been, you could probably tell that the minute you met me. Slippery, shady. Practically criminal, really. She refused to give me your cell number, but she did let slip what company you work for. Forgive me for phoning so late."

"It *is* late. I have to go, my boys are waiting for me."

"Boys! You have boys. How delightful. I love boys. I *was* a boy once, you know. It was wonderful. Boys are wonderful."

"Really, I—"

"Oh, sorry, sorry. I'm babbling. I do that a lot, you'll find that out eventually. Better you know right away than later on, when it's too late. Look, hang up, go fetch your wonderful boys, but I'm going to call you again and we'll talk properly. We have a lot of—"

A lot of what? Laurel would never know, because she hung up.

8

Your Piece of Paradise

It took some time, and she hesitated and questioned herself at first, but once she got into the swing of deciding, Rose kept on going. She chose her colours (no avocado green, no forest green, not a hint of green), picked out tiles (easy), said yes to a new sink and cabinet and no to a new toilet (the current one was white, the sour cream in a room of guacamole), and opted, after long deliberation and detailed online research (performed, proudly, without Laurel's help), for two extra jets below the rain head.

How did she accomplish it all while working extra hours to ready the garden centre for tomorrow's grand opening? Maybe she'd picked up the renovation bug at work and had to let it run its course. Maybe she was powered by the unfamiliar energy that zinged through her whenever she saw Tripp, who worked, lifting the heaviest loads, logging the longest hours, taking no breaks, as intensely as he stared.

However she made it happen, the handyman, Stu, was now here, with his reluctant-looking younger brother in tow. It was a job for two, Stu told her. Might as well keep it in the family.

Finally, she was improving her dated condo. At last, she was yanking one piece from the exhibits of the Seventies Museum. Rose was getting a new bathroom. And, happily, she had saved the money to pay for it.

Home. Few words suggest more warmth, heart, and family feeling. Where and how you live affects every facet of your life. Home gives you emotional security, but if you own the place you live in, home also provides financial security.

We believe that, if you can make it happen, owning your little piece of paradise is better than renting and making someone else's mortgage payments. Real estate tends to be a wise long-term investment if you can swing it. It typically increases in value over time, at a rate at least equal to the rate of inflation. Owning property can boost your net worth, and eventually, once you pay off your mortgage, you'll rid yourself of a large monthly expense.

The same principles that apply to investing in stocks also apply to investing in real estate. It takes time, patience, and discipline to reap the rewards of growth, and you'll want some trusted individuals on hand. The best people to have on your real estate team are a real estate agent, a lawyer or notary, a banker or mortgage broker, and a building inspector.

Not sure if owning property is in the cards for you? We have two words for you: be *flexible* and *creative.*

Look for flexible solutions, even when the odds seem daunting. If real estate is too pricey where you want to live, why not move to a different area—a more affordable part of town, a more affordable city, a more affordable part of the country? Seeing possibilities instead of problems is a valuable skill in investing and in life.

Look for creative solutions, including using real estate creatively. What if you rented out the top floor (or floors) of your house in the early years and *you* lived in the downstairs suite? You'd be maximizing your returns. You could always reverse the setup later after paying off more of the mortgage.

HOME, SWEET HOME OWNERSHIP

First-time real estate buyers often ask us the same things. We'd like to share their questions and our answers with you.

You strongly recommend buying real estate. Why?

Real estate is a *real* asset. You can see it, touch it, paint it, and mow it. Owning real estate is part of having a diversified portfolio.

What research should I do before buying?

It's important to do your homework. Start by making a shopping list of your personal must-have features. Do this before you eyeball what's out there and before emotion takes over. Your list could include things like a full dining room, a fireplace, a quiet street, proximity to schools, and an area with a low crime rate.

Next, consider different areas where you might want to live. Go online and tour open houses to see what's available. Check how much people in the same area are currently asking for similar homes on similar properties.

At some point, you'll probably want a real estate agent to help you with your search, gather recent sale prices, show you properties, and give you advice.

Is there a right time to buy?

People who hold real estate for a long time tend to do well on their investment. If you're in a position to buy, it's probably smart to do it sooner than later, to give your investment the most time possible to grow.

You always have more control buying real estate than you do selling it. Sellers are at the mercy of the market. When you're a buyer, it's easy to figure out how much you want to pay. You can say, "This is my top price. If you don't want it, then you don't have to take my money." We recommend speaking to a real estate agent, who can help you navigate the current market conditions.

How can I afford to buy real estate?
In earlier chapters, we discussed the virtues of goal setting, planning, budgeting, saving, and investing to achieve your hopes and dreams. If home ownership is part of your dream, those steps take on renewed importance now.

If you want to buy a home but aren't sure you can afford it, maybe you need a reality check. Go back to basics. What's a Need and what's a Want? Can you scale down the size and grandeur of the home you'd like?

Be flexible too. Living a little farther out rather than in a pricey central location may bring home ownership within reach. Maybe you can take public transit or carpool to cut costs. Maybe there are other sacrifices you can make to reach your goal.

How much can I borrow?
Your banker or mortgage broker will explain the exact criteria used to determine your eligibility for a mortgage. You'll need to supply accurate financial information so that your lender can figure out the mortgage payments you're capable of making.

As a rule, you should spend no more than 30% of your net income on a mortgage payment. In red-hot markets, you may need to borrow more. Bankers and other mortgage lenders have some flexibility in the borrowing criteria they use, but 30% is a reasonable, conservative guide.

Talk to your lender about the frequency and amount of your mortgage payments. You can save thousands of dollars over the term of a mortgage by adjusting these variables. Weekly or biweekly payments will pay off a mortgage faster than the same amount of money paid monthly. Some lenders will allow you to increase your payment in various ways, again shaving time and cost off the overall mortgage.

Always arrange your financing first, before buying anything. Know how much cash you need for a down payment, how much you can borrow, and how much you can afford to pay on a monthly or biweekly basis.

How much should I borrow?

What you *can* borrow and *should* borrow are two different things. It's important to be sure you can afford what you're getting into.

Be cautious about borrowing as much as you're allowed. If your mortgage rate shoots up, if you or your partner is suddenly out of work, or if you face a surprise expense, like a major home repair, you may not be able to afford the mortgage payments. Many families are house rich and cash poor. The worst thing you can do is put yourself in a position where you *have* to sell your home, possibly at the wrong time.

The cost of buying a home goes well beyond its selling price. You'll face a number of one-time expenses. They may include legal fees, land transfer fees, appraisal costs, any and all applicable taxes, survey fees, home inspection fees, major appliances, moving costs, utility connection fees, repairs, redecorating, and garden equipment.

Don't forget ongoing expenses such as property tax, home insurance, mortgage insurance, life insurance (possibly already built into your mortgage), utility costs, utility taxes, maintenance, and commuting costs. Some types of housing require you to pay homeowners' association fees or condominium fees.

What about renting?

There are a number of circumstances in which renting makes sense.

- If renting allows you to save up a down payment, by all means do it.
- In some global markets (such as London, Hong Kong, New York City, Vancouver), buying a home can be difficult if not impossible for first-time buyers who lack high-paying jobs, wealthy parents, or an inheritance. We recommend renting something you can afford and increasing your savings while you rent.
- Depending on your age, health, and situation in your senior years, you may want to sell the property you own and use your equity in it to improve your cash flow. In that case, renting is not out of the question. It can simplify your life: no major maintenance to worry about, no property taxes, no angst. Your home isn't a piggy bank, but it could become an important resource later in life, when other resources are depleted. It may be the biggest rainy day fund you could ever hope for.
- As you get older, renting can also be good for the orderly transition of your estate. As a tenant, you're responsible only for the rent and for obeying any reasonable rules your landlord may have set. Period. If the owner wants to gamble on an asset whose value could go down as well as up, fine. You don't need to take the same risk with the assets that make up your estate.
- Selling your home and renting may allow you to give loved ones some of your valuable or sentimental belongings while you're still alive. To prevent family disputes later, it's a good idea to record these items and your early disposition of them in writing, then store the document with someone you trust.

If you truly can't afford the mortgage you need, renting may be for you. But there are other options.

One is to buy the home you want, rent it out, and rent a more modest place until you can afford to live in the one you really want. Another is to rent where you need to work and buy where you want to retire. Rent out the retirement property so that someone pays it off for you. A few years from now, when the retirement property is paid off, you'll be a homeowner.

———

Laurel stood in the wide hardwood landing at the top of the curved oak staircase. The arched window opposite framed her favourite view, a grove of giant oaks in the rolling park across the street.

The park was what had clinched the deal for her and Matthew six years ago. Exhausted, they had finally accepted that the boys, who were learning to walk, ran on batteries eternally charged. They were everywhere at once, on top of the footstool, at the sink, under the bed, inside the broom closet, toppling from sofas and chairs. A soft green space just across the street, with no flagstones or patio furniture or barbecues to run into, was about the best thing Laurel and Matthew could imagine.

The two-and-a-half storey Victorian, with a slope-ceilinged attic they could finish one day, teetered at the top of their price range. But they both worked solid jobs—Matthew taught high-school English—and they knew how to live frugally. They threw all their extra money at the mortgage. It didn't amount to much, just a few double-up payments a year, enough to nibble at the principal.

Now there was no extra money. I can't afford it, Laurel told herself, as she did every time she savoured this view. I've got to sell. Pull the money out, find a smaller place, get a mortgage I can afford.

It was the right thing to do, the only way she could manage over the long haul. So many expenses lay ahead. The boys were growing like vines, their sports alone cost a fortune, and she hadn't even started their education funds yet.

It was the right thing to do, she knew it. Her head accepted every argument. But her heart, stubborn troublemaker, rebelled. This house held her to Matthew, to a time when their family was whole, when they had dared to dream and loved to laugh. How could she lose him, lose their future together, then willingly hand over this final trace?

NOT EVERY HOME IS A HOUSE

Economic and population-related pressures are changing our concept of home. If living in the style your parents once did is no longer practical or possible, remember to look for *flexible* solutions. There are some other forms of home ownership out there that you may find more affordable.

Condos

Condominiums come in a variety of styles and sizes and with a variety of amenities. Each condo unit owner has individual title to the space inside the unit. This space is sometimes described as beginning with "the paint on the walls." Each unit owner also has an undivided interest in the physical components of the condominium buildings and land.

Condos used to be mostly popular with young people entering the real estate market and with older people seeking to downsize, free up equity from the family home, and avoid the responsibilities of property maintenance. Times have changed. Condos are now popular with every age and lifestyle, whether as a primary residence, vacation home, or revenue-producing investment.

There are pros and cons to condos. Condos emphasize collective rights that benefit many over individual rights that benefit few. Such decisions may not suit your lifestyle. Owners pay a monthly fee for shared maintenance and repairs. Over time, that fee can rise sharply. The residents elected to oversee the building's maintenance and security must be good at long-term thinking. Otherwise, the building may fall into disrepair, devaluing each unit. Read at least two years' worth of the condo council's reports before you buy. They'll tell you if the complex has a healthy contingency fund for emergencies.

On the upside, a well-managed condo offers a level of flexibility and "lock-and-leave" security that a detached residence may not. Also, a condo usually costs less than a similar detached home in a comparable area. Be aware, however, that a condo's value may not rise as much over time as that of a single detached home.

Co-ops

With co-operative housing, or a co-op, you don't actually own real estate. You own shares in a corporation, and the corporation, in turn, owns the real estate. This is a small but important nuance. The number of shares you buy is equivalent to the portion of the building occupied by your suite. Your shares also give you access to the common property that all owners (or their tenants) share.

When you buy a condominium, the only real issue is that you meet the seller's terms. If you're interested in buying a co-op, the board may interview you first to assess your suitability.

Financing a co-op can be trickier than financing a house or condo. When you buy into a co-op, your financial institution uses your share certificate as collateral. Banks greatly prefer to see a "piece of dirt" as an asset against which to lend money.

Modular, manufactured, or mobile homes

Many people love the "just-right" size, not to mention the price, of modular and mobile homes. But nothing is perfect.

Depending on the development, residents buy or rent their *pad*, the piece of land that the home sits on. The purchase or rental is often costly. We also wonder what happens when the owner-landlord of such a development decides to sell the land. It's expensive to move a modular or mobile home from one location to another, which often makes the value of the unit itself quite nominal.

―――○○○―――

RESIDENTIAL REAL ESTATE TIPS

Know what you want. Remember the basics of budgeting. Make a list of features you Need. Make another list of features you Want. Set a budget and stick to it. Don't spend more than you can afford.

Location, location, location. Ask any real estate agent about the most important feature of a home and that's what you'll hear.

Use retirement savings to buy your first home. Canada allows first-time buyers to dip into their retirement savings to finance a first-time home purchase. Talk to your banker or financial advisor to see if you qualify.

Arrange pre-approved financing. Knowing the money's there when you need it will help you move quickly when making an offer to buy.

Get the best interest rate. Your mortgage broker has access to many lenders and will seek out the best rate for you. If you're dealing with a banker, negotiate the best rate that the lending institution is willing to offer.

Get a building inspection. A certified, experienced home inspector will produce a written report that documents any deficiencies with the property.

Have a notary or lawyer do the title search and property transfer. Protect yourself against fraud by using a qualified professional for the legal aspects of buying and selling.

Make room for a mortgage helper. If your budget is tight, consider adding a basement suite or renting out a room to help pay the mortgage.

Maintain an emergency fund. Keep some money aside for major repairs and other hidden or unexpected costs of home ownership.

Sell your home in the most convenient, efficient way. Many people believe they'll save a bundle by selling their home privately, and some do. However, there are definite advantages to using a real estate agent. A big plus is having a buffer between you and the buyer, which does a lot to reduce your stress.

<hr />

The big day was finally here.

After a week of hard labour and serious overtime, punctuated by the occasional plant mishap and personal meltdown, the Blooming Tulip was throwing open its doors (freshly polished and newly lubricated) for day one of the grand reopening sale. The week-long event would, they all hoped, restore customers' faith in them plus draw new patrons and enough curiosity-seekers to spread the word: the Blooming Tulip was back, better than ever.

Half an hour before opening, Mrs. Birch summoned them all up front. She's resplendent, Rose thought. It was a word she didn't even know she knew until this morning, watching the new owner slide out of her dark blue Tesla and stand a moment, examining the new sign that had been installed, with great effort and many flashlights, just before midnight. Draped in a burnt-orange raw silk shift over a long linen skirt, antique silver gleaming at her ears, throat, and wrists, Mrs. Birch glowed brightly.

Now she stood tall before the staff. "You've worked so hard for this day, every one of you. I am so proud of our team."

A general shuffling and mumbling ensued. A few *thank-you*'s floated up.

"And I'm so proud of our garden centre," she continued. "The Blooming Tulip is not just back in business. With everything we've done, our new look, our bigger inventory, our online ordering, the Master Gardener booth, the landscape design business, we are going to be *the* destination for serious gardeners."

The clapping and cheers echoed off the cement walls and floor. Mrs. Birch smiled and gave a tiny bow. "That's it for the pep talk. Remember, customers come first, if we don't have it we can order it, and we deliver. No limits. Now get out there and wow them."

―⁂―

VACATION PROPERTIES: DREAM CATCHERS OR DUST CATCHERS?

Do your dreams include a vacation home you can call your own? Whether it's a cottage by the lake, a chalet in the mountains, or an oasis in the tropics, we believe you should follow your dreams—as long as they don't turn into nightmares.

Vacation properties, and lifestyle investments such as boats and motorhomes, come with risks as well as rewards. By all means, build a getaway property into your financial plan. Just make sure you know what you're getting into, and be smart about your purchase.

As with buying a home, being smart with vacation property means being flexible and creative. We know a woman who rented out her ski chalet for the first three years she owned it, never *once* staying there herself. She built her equity in two ways: by paying down the mortgage faster and by benefiting from the rise in real estate prices in the economically brisk area where she'd bought. Her small sacrifice paid big dividends—her chalet is now mortgage-free.

When it comes to vacation purchases, one solution doesn't fit all. Our bottom-line advice: If you decide to buy your dream getaway, whatever it is, know the rules of the road, ask common-sense questions, and seek out the wisdom of professionals.

Family cottages and vacation homes

Pleasure comes from the family cottage—and some angst. A family getaway, where you can surround yourself with generations of family and friends, can create precious memories. But family cottages can also lead to friction.

The angst comes when a cottage needs to be shared among your adult children or siblings. What if just two of your three kids want to use the property? What if a child lives in a different part of the country or abroad? What if your kids don't get along? When your parents left you and your sibling the cottage, did they consider that a divorce could cause havoc? Or that when it came to the next generation, it would be challenging to split the pie into increasingly smaller pieces? Half a pie is easy to manage, but if you and your siblings have seven children among you, it can be hard to cut the slices evenly.

If you're contemplating buying or building a vacation home, ask yourself these questions first:

- Do I honestly think I will use it? Will I use it often enough?
- Will I need to give up other travel as a consequence?
- Do I enjoy home maintenance? Or can I find and afford someone to do that part for me?
- Is the property in a safe enough location that I can leave it unoccupied for months at a time?
- Is the location a true getaway, yet still relatively easy to access?
- Does owning a vacation home represent a reasonable percentage of the time and money I want to allot to vacations?
- Is there a realistic opportunity to rent out the cottage to offset my expenses? If so, do I really want someone else using my stuff?
- How do other family members fit in? Do I want the place to be big enough for visitors or just the right size for me?
- If I'm looking at a property in another country, do I know the tax ramifications?
- Have I realistically determined the monthly expenses?

After answering these questions, if you still feel confident you can handle this lifestyle choice, go for it. If you have any doubts about the wisdom of buying, rent first. Renting is a great way to try out different getaway options. Rent a lakeside cottage one year, a Paris apartment another. You may decide that a close-to-home spot with no travel hassles is just what your heart (and schedule) desires.

Timeshares

People who can't afford to buy a vacation property outright sometimes opt for a timeshare. Just keep your wits and your wallet close when you hear a sales pitch extolling a lifetime of sunny vacations. Anything sounds good when you're sitting under a palm tree with a paper umbrella in your drink.

You only have to check the Internet to get a sense of how many people are trying to sell their timeshares through resellers. Buying privately or through a secondary-market reseller can save you thousands of dollars, but be aware that transaction and maintenance fees still apply.

We urge you to think carefully and answer these questions before the suntan lotion and the ink on your purchase both dry:

- Will I have enough vacation time to use my timeshare every year?
- Can I realistically afford to travel there?
- Do I truly love the place I want to buy?
- Will I feel like I'm going to my own holiday home each year?
- Can I handle the annual maintenance fee? Is the fee low enough that it won't detract from the timeshare if I decide to sell later?

If you can answer a definitive yes in all cases, we'll zip our lips right now.

Bottom line? We don't think timeshares are investments. But if the price and terms are right, and you really love the place, go ahead . . . maybe. Enjoy your holidays. Come home with photos and great memories. Just don't leave your common sense behind.

Fractional ownership

When you buy a vacation property, you lay out big bucks and get an asset in exchange. When you buy a timeshare, you make a lifestyle purchase. When you buy *fractional ownership*—one-quarter, one-tenth, or any other partial ownership—of a vacation home or resort, you're getting a hybrid of the two.

With, for example, quarter-ownership, you receive a 25% interest in a deeded property. You'll typically get access to the property twelve or thirteen weeks a year, or one week a month, on a rotational basis. Some weeks no one can use the property, to allow for general maintenance.

The theory is that most people don't use a vacation property enough to justify the expense. In theory, a shared ownership structure is a tidy solution. Fractional ownership can work beautifully, but there are pitfalls. Watch for hefty management fees, rising maintenance fees, tax implications, and finally, the price tag.

Houseboats, motorhomes, and other movable real estate

Some vacation purchases, such as boats and motorhomes, are actually consumables, commodities with a limited lifespan and use. These can be wonderful lifestyle purchases, as long as you take the time to think them through. Is your decision to buy based on logic and reason? Or on head-over-heels, love-at-first-sight emotion?

If you're contemplating movable real estate, keep heart and head in synch. Sure, you'll love cruising the coast in your luxury yacht, but how keen will you be to go boating if your priorities or finances change? And the initial outlay for a boat is just the start. Can your budget handle the insurance, registration, maintenance, moorage, and fuel? If owning a boat is an impractical dream, renting or chartering may be a better option for you.

Whether you're tempted by an RV or a houseboat, consider what it is you're actually buying. How old is the unit? Is it structurally and mechanically sound? If not, can you afford to fix it up? What is its true value, not just in dollars and cents but in terms of the use and enjoyment you can expect from it? Should you rent it instead?

—∞—

Fittingly enough, for people who connect investment and gardening, we like dirt. Real estate can be a great investment in the right circumstances, at the right time, and when all the elements click into place. We believe in home ownership and encourage you to save and plan so that you can purchase your piece of paradise.

A cautionary tip: Don't buy and sell too often. The costs of real estate transactions, including all the expenses of moving, can quickly add up and eat away at the value you've built.

———— ⚬⚬⚬ ————

After Mrs. Birch's speech, Jasmine made a beeline for Rose. "Rosie! You look awesome."

Rose fingered the green and blue silk scarf Laurel had lent her. Apart from it, she wore her own clothes: a pearl-grey blouse with shell buttons, fitted black pants, and, for once, low heels instead of safety shoes. "I'm at the Master Gardener booth today. Mrs. Birch wants me there in case there are any kinks. So till five o'clock I'm a volunteer, not on staff."

"I know you, you'll end up selling a ton of stuff anyway. You've got a way with people."

"Me? The original foot-in-mouth woman? You've got to be joking."

Jasmine shook her head and her beaded braids clacked. "No, I mean it. You've got a soft touch, but it works. You sell more than any of us. I heard Mrs. Birch telling Tripp."

"Tripp?" Rose's pulse raced. "She won't even say hi to him. What were they talking about?"

Jasmine shrugged. "Business, I guess. Oh, and he was married. But it was years and years ago." Rose gaped. "What?" said Jasmine. "I figured you'd want to know. I heard him tell Marcus."

"So what, are you the resident spy now?"

"I can't help it if I happen to be in the right place at the right time. It's good info, right? Listen, can I borrow thirty bucks? Just till Friday."

"Here we go. I thought you had a sugar dad— I mean, a sugar person." Then Rose's face collapsed. "Oh, no, honey. Did you break up?"

"Not at all. We're not even officially a couple or anything. It's just, I've got my pride, you know? It's my turn to treat. That's why I need thirty."

Where was Jasmine going to find a date-worthy dinner for two for thirty bucks, even a vegan dinner of nuts and sprouts? Rose handed over two bills.

"That's forty."

"Ten of it's a gift." Jasmine began to speak but Rose held up a hand. "Believe me, I won't make a habit of it. I just want your evening to go well. But listen." She dropped her voice. "You need to think about getting a real job, something full-time that actually supports you. Or you've got to spend less. You can't keep staying at other people's places and living off other people's cash."

Jasmine's mouth quivered. "I— But it's *hard*. There's always something. I've got to eat out, it's not like I have a kitchen. There's clothes. Then there's the club, you've got to buy drinks or they'll kick you out. And then Sadie got way behind on her rent, so I had to lend her a bunch. I always pay you back."

"I know you do. It's not about that. It's about—" Rose searched for the right way to say it. "It's about looking ahead, and taking care of yourself. You're such a free spirit, you like to go your own way. That's a wonderful thing, but you need to be independent in other ways too, stand on your own two feet."

"Rose." It was a man's voice. Tripp's voice. Just like that, Rose's words vanished.

He stood, hands hooked in the back pockets of his slim jeans, and smiled briefly, a flash of white in his tanned face. He smelled of soap and earth. "You look nice today," he said. And you are the most gorgeous man I've ever seen in real life, she thought. "I'm starting on that garden next week. That British guy's place. My first big contract." He touched her arm. "I have you to thank for it."

Rose stood, trembling slightly, and watched Tripp walk away. Jasmine watched Rose.

"You tell *me* to stand on my own two feet," Jasmine said. "Every time that guy comes within shouting distance, you can hardly stand up at all." She smirked. "You got it bad, Rosie. Real bad."

Part Three: Tending

9

Our Seven Investment Beliefs

Two weeks, fourteen days, 336 hours. That's how long Rose had been washing her face and brushing her teeth over the kitchen sink and taking showers at Laurel's after work. Two weeks of tiptoeing around sections of pipe, buckets of grout and drywall, and piles of new tiling to get to the toilet, thankful every time that she'd elected to keep that essential fixture. Two weeks of phoning Stu, every day at first, less often now that the realization was sinking in.

Stu had disappeared. He'd worked three days, long enough to tear out the old tub, sink, and cabinet and—for this Rose truly gave thanks—cart them to the dump. On the third morning he arrived alone, subdued, the whereabouts of his sullen brother a mystery Rose never got to the bottom of before heading to the Blooming Tulip. The good news was she hadn't paid him up front.

The last she saw of Stu, he was prying tiles off the wall and humming to himself. The tune was vaguely familiar. An old, sad blues song.

───── ∞∞∞ ─────

Now that you know more about the kinds of investments out there, and the risks and rewards associated with each, you're nearly ready to start planting your money.

First, however, we'd like to share with you some guiding principles. Every day, as we manage people's money and their financial futures, we rely on seven core beliefs about investing. Most of these beliefs we've already touched on in this book. Because all seven are important, not only to us, but to you as you plant your financial garden, we'd like to gather them together here.

We believe:

1. Ownership builds wealth.
2. Your money should work for you.
3. Investing is long-term and saving is short-term.
4. You can't time the market.
5. Chasing returns rarely works.
6. You shouldn't be afraid to sell your stock.
7. Good financial advice is essential.

1. Ownership builds wealth

It's a myth that to create wealth, you need to make a lot of money at your job. While that helps, it's not entirely necessary. If you can save 10% to 20% of your income each year, in ten years you'll have saved one to two years' average salary. That's just a start.

There are three basic ways to create wealth: investing in your own business as an entrepreneur, investing in other well-run businesses, and investing in real estate. All three ways are similar in that with each, you're buying a different form of equity. Equity equals ownership. Over time, good-quality equity tends to increase in value.

When we ask wealthy people how they amassed their fortune, if not through inheritance or a lottery win, they rarely just say that they saved their money. They say that they saved their money and *invested it* over their lifetime. You don't earn as much on savings as you do on equity. Money in the bank or in short-term, safe investments grows very slowly. Equity tends to grow more.

Investing in equity gives you the chance to earn a higher return than you could in term deposits, GICs, or bonds. That isn't true every year, because markets sometimes goes down, but history shows that over a 20-year time frame, equities outperform other asset classes, such as real estate and bonds. That's why we believe equity builds wealth. Be an owner.

2. Your money should work for you

As we've said before, it all starts with discipline and a plan. You have to set goals and follow a plan of action to reach them. As we've also said, it's the small spending choices you make each day—taking a packed lunch to work instead of eating out, making coffee at home or the office instead of buying it at a cafe—that determine how much money you can save for the future.

Yet if you let your savings languish in a bank account or term deposit, earning next to nothing, you'll actually lose money because inflation will eat away at the value each year. You need to get that money working for you.

The key to growing your wealth is to pay attention to your annual return. Even a small increase in your average annual return can make a huge difference to your net worth.

Let's say, for illustration purposes, you deposit $10,000 into a tax-sheltered account and allow your investment to grow over 20 years. If you were to earn 2% per year, reinvesting the earnings so that they compound over time, your investment would grow to nearly $15,000. The problem, as we discussed in Chapter 7, is inflation. The average inflation rate over the same time frame has likely been 2% or more. That means the spending power of the $10,000 you invested 20 years ago has actually *decreased*.

Maybe you do a little better and earn 4% per year on the same invest-ment. To keep the return consistent, let's say you buy a 20-year bond that pays you 4% each and every year. Now, with compounding, your $10,000 will produce $22,000 in 20 years. That's a much better number than the $15,000 in the previous example. You've likely taken on more risk to get the higher return, but probably not too much risk if you're getting only 4% per year. In this example, you've doubled your money and then some. That's the kind of investment that can work for you, because there's mean-ingful growth beyond the inflation rate.

Let's do a little more math. Say you invest $10,000 in stocks and let it sit for 20 years. Over that time, you earn 6% per year and allow your money to compound. Can you guess how much your $10,000 will grow over 20 years? At 6%, your original $10,000 becomes $32,000.

Now imagine this. You invest $4,000 a year over 30 years and earn an average of 6% per year. In 30 years, you'll have $316,232. If you increase your investment to $5,000 a year, you'll have $474,349. These are serious amounts of money.

In all these sample scenarios, the earlier you start, the more consistent you are at putting money away, and the higher your average annual return, the more money you'll have. That's why we believe your money should work for you.

3. Investing is long-term and saving is short-term

If you're saving money to retire in a decade or two, you have time on your side and should invest a good chunk of your money in equities. If you're saving for something like a home or a car and your time frame is much shorter, say one or two years, you should put your money in the bank or in a term deposit to keep it safe. We advise you to do that because the stock market fluctuates every day, every week, and every year.

Equities are a great investment over time, but anything can happen in the short term. You can easily lose money because you need cash at a specific time and have to sell when the market is down. True, you can get lucky. You may invest when the market is weak, when it's possible to earn great returns in a year or two. But if you're not lucky and the timing isn't right, you can defeat the very purpose of saving by losing the money you need.

To invest well, you have to commit your funds to a long-term horizon, at least five to seven years and ideally more than ten. Over time, the market goes up more than it goes down, but the key to that statement is *over time*.

The more time you have, the better. Many people want to make a quick buck. They don't have the patience to let their money grow. That's why they find it hard to make money in the stock market. Most people buy real estate with a long-term outlook, knowing they'll probably lose money if they sell in the short term. Why should things be different when you invest in a business? That's why we believe investing is long-term and saving is short-term.

⊶⊷

Laurel hung up. She'd done the right thing: booked three real estate agents to appraise her house. Her heart sank with every call, but what choice did she have? Physically, she couldn't work more than she already did. If she didn't sell the house, she'd soon have to dip into her retirement savings, something she vowed never to do. *That's buried gold*, as her father would say. *Don't dig it up till your golden years.*

Her father. He would help her if she asked, especially now that he'd sold his accounting firm and lived in a modest farmhouse on the east coast. He'd offer a low interest rate too. Not *no* interest rate—he was too shrewd a businessman for that—but he would undercut the banks. She had wavered recently, but in the end dismissed the idea. Taking money from her father only meant more debt. She needed to put debt behind her.

Her fifteen-minute break must be over. Glancing at the time on her phone, she saw that she'd missed a call while on the line with the real estate agent. The number made her smile. After three weeks she knew it well, and these days it provoked more amusement than annoyance. It was—she checked her notebook—the fourth call since yesterday from her tireless British suitor. She wasn't keeping an Excel spreadsheet this time, but she was counting. "I need the numbers," she told her friend Jenny, who had heard many of Al's rambling, hilarious messages. "What can I say? I have my father's genes."

Lately, if Al phoned when she wasn't in the middle of something, she actually answered instead of letting the call go to voicemail. His humour, his irrepressible energy and, she had to admit, his insane yet dogged belief that she would one day consent to go out with him lifted her spirits.

Three minutes of her break left. Should she? She had never called him before. Would it send the wrong message? After all, she had no intention of seeing him. None at all.

He picked up on the first ring. "This is your accountant," she announced. "I've gone through the books, and you're up to phone call number thirty. After that, I charge double."

---

4. You can't time the market

Trying to figure out what the stock market will do in the short term is a difficult guessing game. There are many factors and uncertainties that can move the market in either direction.

Markets have a way of surprising everyone. They can and do behave irrationally at times, even opposite to what you might expect. Unpredictable global events certainly play a role, but even if you see them coming, you may not know how the market will react.

We believe that it's not timing the market, but *time in* the market that creates wealth. If you wait for conditions to be perfect before you jump in, you're shortening the long-term horizon that's so important for sound investing.

Remember Chapter 2 and the Paralysis by Analysis investment personality? There are always reasons not to invest in the market. Each day seems to bring bad news, whether it's a natural disaster, a looming financial crisis, or a war halfway around the world.

After the frightening events of September 11, 2001, when two planes crashed into the World Trade Center in New York, the US markets closed for six days. In the first few days after the reopening, the Standard & Poors 500 Index dropped by 18%.

In 2010, the petroleum industry's largest-ever ocean oil spill killed eleven people, wreaked havoc with marine and wildlife habitats, and dealt a blow to tourism in the Gulf of Mexico. Shares of BP plunged to less than half their previous value.

In 2011, Japan briefly closed its stock markets following the country's magnitude 9.0 earthquake and subsequent tsunami, and the nuclear crisis that followed. On average, uranium stocks fell 25% amid fears of a nuclear meltdown.

Although no one could predict these huge events, what is predictable is that markets dislike uncertainty. Markets react and markets calm down, and then, as other crises occur, the cycle repeats itself. Trying to time the market is crazy-making. Carefully considered, balanced, diversified investments stand the test of time.

5. Chasing returns rarely works

When you see a stock shoot up, you may think about jumping in. The business looks good, investor confidence is high, and others are making money, so why shouldn't you? But by the time you get in, the stock is already expensive because it's been rising, and your purchase fuels that rise even further. This is called *chasing returns*—buying because everyone else is buying.

Along the same lines, some people chase money managers, always on the lookout for the top-ranked manager, moving from one person or firm to the next. It's almost a curse when an advisor wins the Manager of the Year award, because rarely can any professional maintain a consistent number-one level of performance. No investment style works every single year. An individual money manager's performance is likely to wax and wane somewhat over the years.

The point? Markets and strategies change all the time. You can't expect to own the number-one stock or have the number-one money manager every time. The more you try to chase those disappearing targets, the more you're likely to stray from your well-ordered plan. Building wealth depends more on consistent performance in the long term than on star performance in the short term.

If you try to follow each and every swing, you'll be in for a roller-coaster ride. We've seen it. We believe it. That's why we believe chasing returns rarely works.

6. You shouldn't be afraid to sell your stock

We can't tell you how often we sit down with clients to suggest changes to their portfolios only to hear, "I'd like to keep this stock awhile. I don't want to sell it now. Let's just watch it." When we ask why, the answers include:

"The stock is down from where I bought it." "I don't want to lose money on it." "I think it'll keep going up." Or the classic "I just like owning it."

Many people make the mistake of clinging to a stock for too long. We've touched before on the emotional attachment some people have to their investments. But we want you to understand and remember this, so we're saying it again: *Don't let emotion cloud a sound business rationale for selling.*

It's easy to buy a stock. You hope your timing is perfect, and you imagine the share price rising beyond belief. Good things are sure to happen. But sometimes—quite often, actually—your timing isn't perfect and the stock drops below what you paid for it.

In many cases, there's nothing to worry about. You can and should hold the stock and collect your dividend income while waiting for the share price to rise over time. In other cases, however, something unexpected happens. The company loses business to a competitor. Future earnings look as though they'll fall over time. The share price seems overvalued. A key person has left and the replacement doesn't instill confidence. Developments like these suggest that the share price will fall, or fall further, and they're good reasons to sell or reduce your position.

Why else would you sell a stock? Your advisor may suggest reducing a position that has grown considerably. Your portfolio may need rebalancing. There may be tax concerns.

What it comes down to is that when the situation changes, you need to change with it or risk being left behind. Don't let emotions get the better of you and lead you to reject a carefully considered plan. No one likes selling at a loss and no one likes to be proven wrong, but in some cases, selling is the right thing to do. That's why we believe you shouldn't be afraid to sell your stock.

7. Good financial advice is essential

Investing is difficult; making a mistake when investing is easy. Everyone makes a wrong choice at some point—picks a bad stock, sells too early, sells too late. If the world's best money managers make mistakes now and again, so will you.

Even if you're very competent about managing your finances—you're not swayed by volatile swings in the market, you're patient, you don't get emotionally attached to your stocks, you've never even mildly panicked and sold off in fear (we're pretty sure we've eliminated most people by now)—having someone as a source of new ideas, or to bounce your own ideas off of, is invaluable.

If you work with someone you can trust throughout your entire life, you'll have the best possible chance of getting the most from your investment portfolio. It's that simple. That's why we believe good financial advice is essential.

———

In this chapter, and throughout this book, we urge you to save, invest, and build equity. This is not empty advice that we're taking from some course or textbook and passing along to you. It's advice that we believe in and use, day in and day out, year after year.

We know, because we see it with our clients: The earlier in life you start to make smart choices, the more smart choices you'll have later in life.

———

"I can't take it anymore. I want my bathroom back." Rose peered morosely at the cheese, tomato, and cucumber sandwich she had assembled that morning beside the kitchen sink, still the only source of running water in her apartment.

"You sure he's not coming back? This handyman guy?" Jasmine plunged her fork into soba noodle salad from the vegetarian cafe down the street. Twelve bucks plus tax, thought Rose, plus another eight for the organic fruit smoothie and who knows how much for the giant muesli cookie. Jasmine owed her sixty dollars now, her highest tab ever, even though the girl was getting full-time hours at the garden centre. Business hadn't slowed since the grand reopening. The Blooming Tulip was blooming and then some.

"He's really gone," said Rose. "His number's disconnected. Listen, Laurel asked me to babysit after work. She's got some evening meeting. I'm ... Well, I can't do it after all. Could you?" Maybe sending extra work Jasmine's way would help the girl more than another unasked-for lecture about budgeting.

Jasmine shrugged. "Sure, I'll bail you out. I'm no good at installing showers and sinks, though. You're on your own there."

"Mind if I join you?" Tripp slid onto the picnic table seat beside Jasmine.

"I thought you were off designing gardens," the girl said.

"Nope. I've got a day between projects. Thought I'd check out the home turf." He unwrapped his sandwich—roast beef on whole wheat, Rose noticed, envious—and busied himself with a mustard packet. "So you need a shower and sink installed?"

Jasmine beat her to it. "This handyman guy just walked out on her three weeks ago, in the middle of the job. Her bathroom's a mess and she can't stand it anymore."

He looked at Rose. That steady, unblinking gaze unsettled her every time. "That so?"

Rose nodded.

"Well, you're in luck."

"Why?" She dropped her head, nudged a shred of cucumber. Even after weeks of watching him come and go, exchanging pleasantries every so often, she could not look at this man for more than a few seconds at a time.

"I know someone, a contractor, specializes in bathrooms. At least, he used to."

"Oh? Who?"

Tripp picked up a napkin, and she lifted her eyes.

"You're looking at him."

10

Life Changes

"Thanks again. Especially for getting the boys to eat the broccoli, not just hurl it at each other. That takes some doing." Laurel handed Jasmine two crisp twenties. "You must be socking it away. That's eighty from me this week alone."

Jasmine laughed. "Nah, not me. Just ask your mom. I get it, I spend it, or else I give it to my friend Sadie. She's always broke. Your mom gives me a hard time about it."

I'd like to give Mom a hard time, Laurel thought. The only reason she was forking over so much money to Jasmine was that suddenly, after years of babysitting regularly, her mother couldn't get free after work. That Tripp person was finishing her bathroom in the evenings, but why couldn't she just leave him there while she watched the boys at Laurel's? Or why couldn't she keep the boys with her at the apartment? Her mom didn't even shower at Laurel's in the evenings anymore. Instead, she popped by in the mornings before work.

"I just don't see the point of saving," Jasmine was saying. "I mean, no offence, but there's a lot more to life than owning stuff. It's about the experiences you have, and the people. Not the stuff. Not for me, anyway."

"True. But there are a lot more experiences out there if you've got a little money tucked away. Not to mention, it's easier to have a place to live, have kids." Laurel looked toward the boys' room, where the twins were making car sounds.

"Maybe one day." Jasmine picked up her shoulder bag and yoga mat. "I kinda like not being tied down."

"Yoga, huh?"

"Yeah, there's a late class. I love it, especially the deep breathing part. I get all blissed out. You do yoga?"

"I wish." Laurel sighed. "I hardly have time for lunchtime cardio anymore. That's the workout I need the most, for the boost. Otherwise it's hard to keep working. I start fading at five-thirty, six o'clock."

Jasmine gave her a strange look. "Well, yeah."

"I always wanted to try yoga, though. Maybe when I'm retired. Okay, off you go. I've got to get those rascals into bed and get some work done." She patted her laptop case. "The evening shift."

❧

As the old saying goes, the only constant in life is change. Change affects everyone, in ways large and small, happy and sad, anticipated and unexpected. Even when it brings good things your way, change can be a difficult process. How you deal with and adapt to change matters tremendously. It can make the difference between a positive outcome and one you'll never recover from.

Once you've planted a garden, you can't simply walk away and leave it be. A garden changes constantly, as does the environment around it.

Regular tending—pruning, weeding, fertilizing, dividing—is a must. So too, your financial plan needs regular attention. When your circumstances or priorities change, your plan needs to change with them.

What if you lose your job or your health fails? What if you divorce or remarry? What if a windfall comes your way? As you know, your financial plan depends on your cash flow, the money that comes in and the money that goes out. If a life change alters that cash flow, you'll need to adjust your plan.

Our advice when the winds of change blow?

Be flexible. If you're headed for a cliff, change direction. Don't let fear or inertia keep you plodding over the edge. No matter how much you prepare for change, you can never anticipate every turn of events. Be ready and willing to change course when life demands it.

Be disciplined. Review your budget and your plan every year or so. Check what's coming in, what's going out, what's left to save. Even if nothing dramatic is happening in your life, you may find that some tweaks are in order. A few small changes here and there can add up to a big change over time.

Have faith. Have faith in your plan. A lot of work and good sense have gone into it. Have faith in your team. You don't have to weather change alone. Above all, have faith in yourself. You can't control all of life's changes, but you can control how well you deal with them.

───✖───

JOB LOSS

A sudden loss of income is one of the most troubling reasons to update your financial plan. It's also one of the most common. Losing a job is something many people have gone through, often unexpectedly and through no fault of their own.

When your income suddenly stops, expenses can add up quickly. As soon as your credit card balances and line of credit start growing, your savings plan will likely stop. The money in your emergency fund can help (we sincerely hope you *have* an emergency fund), but it will last only so long. It can take months, even years, to find a job that replaces your old one.

It's hard to save money at the best of times, but you don't want it to dwindle away at the worst of times. Heavy damage to your savings could have a major impact on your financial plan. Remember, your plan is a long-term commitment. It should be able to accommodate some flux during periods of change. So what can you do?

Waiting for the perfect new job may not be realistic. Work at something to pay the bills. Keep busy. Take advantage of government-sponsored programs that help unemployed people improve their education. Look closely at your budget and trim your expenses. The cutbacks don't need to last forever, just until you get a job that pays enough to maintain the lifestyle you're used to.

SERIOUS ILLNESS OR DISABILITY

No one thinks it will happen to them—except that it can and sometimes does. We know a number of people who have had to quit work because of a stroke, concussion, serious illness, or serious accident. Without insurance, which we'll talk about shortly, bills pile up fast.

Act fast

Look at the cash flow section of your plan, or simply look at your bank statements and credit card statements, to see how much you spend in a three-month period. This will give you an idea of how fast your savings will disappear.

Now, take action. You'll need an action plan to move forward. Look hard at your cash flow and reduce spending wherever you can. Cut and cut again to make sure you don't seriously damage your financial plan.

How and where you live is often your largest monthly expense. If you're renting, consider moving to a cheaper place for a while. If you own a home, you may want to take in a boarder, or lease out part of your home and live in a basement suite, or lease out your entire home and rent an apartment.

A vehicle is often your next-largest expense. It may be cheaper to take it off the road, reducing your driver's insurance to storage insurance only. Taking public transit may cut your costs. Bicycling and walking are great options too, depending on your physical condition.

We aren't suggesting you live like a pauper, but the stress of not earning an income and seeing your savings disappear can be hard to cope with and can slow your recovery. Only *you* can strike the right balance as you accept the challenges of illness or disability.

Insure yourself
Expect the best and prepare for the worst—that's wise planning.

A brief illness or injury may not cause a financial crisis, but a major event can cut a career short. When illness or disability strikes at a young age, there's little or no time to build a nest egg. The monthly cost of care workers, medicine, and equipment can be huge. You'll still need to pay rent or mortgage and put food on the table, and if you have children to care for, the situation is harder yet. It's almost impossible to make do without financial help.

Insuring yourself against accidents, illness, and disability can make a world of difference—to you and your family.

Disability insurance. Serious health problems—from life-threatening conditions to job-related injuries to sickness caused by stress and burnout—can affect anyone at any time. We hope you're one of the lucky ones untouched by illness. But if it does happen, what's your plan?

Your employer may have a disability insurance plan that you can participate in. If not, or if you're self-employed, we cannot stress enough the need for disability insurance. We feel it's the most important type of insurance, outweighing even life insurance, which we'll touch on in Chapter 13. Because it provides a *living benefit*, disability insurance can make the difference between living a comfortable life or a worried existence.

Disability insurance is expensive because the odds that you'll need it are high. On average, one in three people will face at least one disabling accident or illness that lasts 90 days or longer before they're 65 according to the Great-West Life Assurance Company (www.greatwestlife.com). What's more, the average length of a disability that lasts longer than 90 days is almost three years. These time spans represent a considerable amount of work and income missed.

Travel medical insurance. We know a retired woman who, on her honeymoon cruise, suddenly fainted. Diagnosis? Brain tumour. Her insurance company flew the newlyweds to the nearest hospital, where a team of doctors operated to save the woman's life. Weeks later, when she was able to travel, a medical escort accompanied the couple on the long flight home.

A health crisis can hammer your life at any time, including when you're travelling. The woman we know thought she was in perfect health. Even so, she had medical insurance. Without it, she and her husband would have faced a financial nightmare.

Critical illness insurance. This is a relative newcomer to the insurance world. If you have critical illness insurance and are later diagnosed with a disease that's on the insurance company's list, you'll receive a lump sum according to the terms of your policy. If you're unexpectedly diagnosed with cancer, for example, and are insured for $50,000, the insurer will write you a cheque for that amount. Note that you don't have to die to receive the payment.

Before buying critical illness insurance, read the policy carefully. If you have a pre-existing medical condition and it recurs, you may not get a payout.

There's a place for critical illness insurance, but only after the more essential disability and medical policies are in place. If you have room in your budget, consider looking at this newer type of coverage.

<hr>

Six-thirty, half an hour past closing time, Mrs. Birch and Rose were the only ones still at the garden centre.

"Are you sure that's the right total?"

Rose nodded.

A few days ago, Mrs. Birch had asked Rose if she'd be willing to oversee the daily cash. Mrs. Birch would train her. "Other fish to fry," said the regal woman, her only explanation for handing off the task.

"Well, then." Mrs. Birch lowered her reading glasses to the tip of her nose. "That calls for a celebration. Can I take you out to dinner?"

Rose hesitated. Was Mrs. Birch being serious? Why would she treat Rose? What were they celebrating anyway? And what about Tripp and the bathroom?

Apparently Mrs. Birch not only turned around businesses but read minds. "Just say yes, Rose. We've racked up our highest daily sales ever, and it's not even the weekend. We're twenty percent over my projections overall, and they were ambitious to begin with. There's every reason to celebrate. And Lawrence will be fine on his own. He has a key, I presume?"

Rose blushed and nodded. It was official, then. Everyone knew that Tripp was finishing her bathroom. "I am paying him," she said. "He's not doing me a favour or anything."

"I know you're paying him, dear. Though I suspect you are doing *him* a favour."

DEATH OF A LIFE PARTNER

The death of a partner is one of life's hardest hits. It's a time of emotional chaos and confusion. It's also a time to have faith in others—family, friends, and trusted professionals who will put your best interests first, such as a grief counsellor, tax accountant, lawyer, and financial advisor.

As emotionally tumultuous as it can be to lose the one you love, it can be financially difficult as well. At the very least, you'll have financial tasks to take care of and money decisions to make. At worst, your existing financial plan could be derailed. Either way, losing your life partner means your financial plan will have to change.

Be prepared

It helps tremendously if you know where you stand before the emotional tsunami hits. As we'll discuss in Chapter 13, one of the most important personal documents both you and your partner can have, in life and in death, is an up-to-date will. Dying *intestate* (with no written will), can lead to tax nightmares, financial distress, delays, and frustration.

You and your partner also need to know how one another's pension plans work, what government benefits you're entitled to, and whether your retirement savings can be transferred tax-free when one of you dies. If the unexpected happens, you'll want to have a plan so that you aren't forced to move suddenly or make other drastic changes at a time when you may need the comfort of familiar surroundings.

In most tax jurisdictions, the death of a partner, especially if it's a first partner, is fairly simple to handle administratively. Often, the assets you've accumulated together will neatly roll from joint ownership into your name. But make sure, as you accumulate assets during your lives together, that you don't inadvertently set things up in a way that creates a lack of clarity or an outright problem. Be careful whose name is on what. We've seen people forced to pay unnecessary taxes because an asset's ownership structure was unclear or incorrect.

If you're the executor of your partner's estate, learn about your duties *before* you are in crisis. As executor, you'll have obligations not only to yourself but to other beneficiaries, the tax department, and various government agencies. You do have the option of seeking professional help for some or all of the tasks required to settle an estate.

Review your lifestyle and your plan

Losing your life partner can dramatically affect your lifestyle and your income. You may suddenly have to shoulder the household and financial responsibilities formerly shared by two.

We urge you not to make any hasty decisions. These include moving from your home, dating or remarrying too quickly, or allowing adult children to take charge of your affairs unless you want them to. Even then, seek a second opinion from a trusted friend or professional. We've seen Mom uprooted halfway across the country because a well-meaning child couldn't bear the idea of her living alone. But without her existing network of friends and support, Mom may find it harder than ever to cope with her loss. Such good intentions can have disastrous results.

Once your partner's estate is settled, you'll need to revisit your financial plan. We know this will be hard. You may make some false starts and be temporarily unable to continue. But it's crucial that, as soon as you can, you take control of your situation. No matter what your age, your household income and lifestyle will be in for a change. Your budget and your plan will need to change accordingly. You'll also need a new will. We'll talk more about that in Chapter 13.

Remember, the members of your team are there to help. When reviewing your financial future, seek advice from your senior banker, financial planner, lawyer, or notary.

DIVORCE

It's a sobering and oft-cited fact: roughly half of North American marriages end in divorce. Divorce typically causes severe upheaval, emotional and financial alike. If your marriage or life partnership looks like it's going south, stay calm and think smart.

Pre-divorce: act early

Talk to your banker right away, before the situation deteriorates further. If you do divorce, suddenly *you* will be responsible for *you*. That's a big change for many people. Couples tend to build their finances together over the course of their relationship, doing little or nothing individually. As you start talking divorce, you'll want to take some steps toward financial independence, and your banker can help.

Set up bank accounts, credit cards, and (if you need them and you qualify) a mortgage and line of credit, all in your name. If you can't take some of these steps until the divorce proceeds and you reach a settlement, move forward as soon as you're able.

If you and your partner have joint bank accounts, credit cards, lines of credit, or loans, be careful. Unless you have a "prenup" or separation agreement that states otherwise, any signatory to a joint chequing or savings account can withdraw all the money it contains. Ask your banker's advice as soon as possible. You don't want your partner emptying a joint account, or racking up debt on a joint line of credit which you're part-owner of and liable for the repayment.

Post-divorce: take stock

If your relationship ends in divorce, you'll need to stand back and take personal and financial inventory. A lot has changed, and things may change further, but it's important to assess your situation *now*. When so much in your life is different, it's easy to lose sight of your long-term goals and your financial plan. But this is exactly when you need to embrace change and take control.

Pay your banker another visit, or talk to your financial advisor. Has divorce left you in a negative position? Ask whether you should consolidate your debts. Work on a strategy to repay your creditors over time. Talk about re-establishing your credit rating. These steps are integral to your financial plan and your financial future.

With your assets divided, you may have less to live on and may need to move. The cost of running a household doesn't drop by half when one adult lives there instead of two.

Having dependent children at home complicates things further. If you've been a stay-at-home parent, you may need to take a job. Issues such as spousal support, child custody, and the division of property and debt can make it tough to put anything extra into savings.

Once you're on your own, it's more important than ever to get organized and review your budget. If the task feels overwhelming, ask for help.

Divorce raises other questions. What happens to your joint education savings plans? How will your government pension benefits be affected? Will you, as a single person or parent, qualify for extra tax credits and deductions? Talking to your financial planner or advisor is a good starting point for addressing such issues and getting your life back on track.

This is also the time to review your designated beneficiaries. Once you're divorced, you probably won't want any of your estate to pass to your former partner. But it can and does happen, often to the detriment of current partners and children. We know of a woman who was divorced for more than a decade, remarried, and forgot to change the beneficiary on her life insurance policy. When she died, the payout went to her former spouse.

Take the time to review the beneficiary information on your insurance policies, annuities, health savings accounts, RRSPs and other retirement accounts, tax-free savings accounts, and any other important financial assets. You'll also want to update any powers of attorney, living wills, revocable trusts, and other directives—and, of course, your will, which we'll talk about more in Chapter 13.

The duck breast with red currant and orange reduction tasted more delicious than anything Rose had eaten in years. When had she last dined in a good restaurant? Somewhere along the line she and Frank had stopped going out on their birthdays and anniversaries, opting for takeout instead, or, in their last couple of years together, nothing special at all.

She patted her lips with the thick napkin and took a deep breath. "Why did you say that I'm doing Tripp a favour?"

Mrs. Birch set down her fork, which so far appeared not to have touched food. Her long white hair was twisted up tonight, held with a heavy silver comb. Her face looked longer, leaner; her cheekbones stood out like blades. Once again Rose thought how beautiful she was.

"I'm not sure why I said it." As he passed, Mrs. Birch smiled at their waiter, who had greeted her by name earlier. Then she turned back to Rose. "Oh, to heck with that. I know exactly why I said it. He is sweet on you."

Heat flamed in Rose's cheeks. She must have misheard. "Why?— I mean, how— What do you mean?"

"I guess no one uses that expression nowadays. I mean he is keen on you, he fancies you, you have captured his eye."

"But—"

"Come, Rose. You know very well what I mean. Don't tell me you haven't noticed."

Rose shook her head. She was dumbfounded, completely and utterly.

"Well, it's perfectly apparent. Whenever he's at the garden centre, even if he's just popping in for supplies, the first thing he does is find you. He doesn't say anything usually, but he hangs around and he watches you. There's only one thing that makes a man do that."

"But, but—you don't like him." Mrs. Birch raised a hand as if to protest, but Rose kept on. "It's not just me saying this. We all know it. You're so cold to him. It's like you don't trust him."

Mrs. Birch took a sip of water. "Well, I didn't like him, that much is true. Not at first. And I wasn't sure if I trusted him."

What about now? Rose longed to ask, but she feared the answer. She could no longer deny her feelings for Tripp. Every evening that he showed up at her apartment, and went quietly and steadily to work, she felt closer to him. She couldn't say why. They talked no more than they did at work, yet his presence permeated every square inch of her home, filled every molecule of her mind.

Mrs. Birch's distaste for Tripp was the fence that kept Rose at a distance. Be careful, she kept telling herself. There's something about him. Your boss is the smartest, most successful woman you've ever met. She knows something about him. She *knows*.

Now that we've covered some of the negative changes that can alter your life financially and emotionally, let's talk about life events that are usually positive. Thankfully, there are many.

NEW LIFE PARTNER

Are you about to commit to a lifetime relationship? Have you decided to live with someone or get married? Congratulations to you both. It's a wonderful thing when two people find each other and decide to share their lives. Whether it's your first partnership or a subsequent one, planning a life together can be exhilarating. We'd like to emphasize the *planning* part.

When you say yes to a life partner, your dreams for a happy future together should include plans for your financial future. Where do you both stand? Are you coming into the relationship with separate financial plans? Or no financial plans? No matter how diligent (or lax) you've been about money as individuals, now that you're going to share a home and a life, you need to review your situation together.

Take some time to talk about finances and come to some agreements. Discuss spending and saving, decide on a budget, set goals you both want to work toward. Revisit your individual financial plans, if you have them. Do they still make sense? Or do you need a strategy for two? Your financial advisor can help you create a plan that will take you both where you want to go.

Domestic partnership agreements

Many people who contemplate marriage or remarriage want protection if the marriage breaks down. That's particularly so if they're bringing assets and children into a second or subsequent relationship.

No matter how much you love and trust your partner, you'll want some kind of domestic agreement. A legal agreement protects you and those you love by shielding your assets.

Prenuptial, postnuptial, and other domestic partnership agreements define the financial arrangement between partners before, during, and after the partnership. The agreements vary greatly depending on jurisdiction. They generally include obligations for both parties. Some agreements require the full financial disclosure of all assets (including business interests), liabilities, and income. Some include guidelines for how children will be raised. Note that neither you nor your partner can eliminate your obligations to your children by a simple agreement.

Whatever domestic agreement you enter into, make sure it's legally crafted by someone experienced in the field. And make sure that both you and your partner get independent legal advice. It's important that there is no suggestion of coercion or undue influence by one or both of you.

Second or subsequent partners

Second and subsequent partnerships can bring with them complex inheritance issues, especially if there are no wills.

The exact issues depend on your individual situation and jurisdiction. Children from a prior marriage, yours or your partner's, can be unintentionally excluded if a new will hasn't been made or has been poorly drafted. If one of you dies, the surviving partner may be unwilling to provide for the adult children of the deceased partner unless legal documentation requires it.

If you're remarrying or committing to someone new, especially if either of you has children from a previous relationship, be sure to sit down with a professional and draft a will that addresses situations like these.

NEW CHILD

Babies are a joy. They will change your life forever. They're also expensive. Whether you're having your first child or growing your existing family, try to build babies into your financial plan early, while they're still a glimmer in your eye instead of an infant in your arms. Start saving now so that your money grows over time.

A new child brings a lot of costs and a lot of changes. Review your budget and your plan regularly to make sure you stay on track. Review or update your will as soon as possible to make sure your new child is covered. And don't forget higher education. If you think it is expensive now, imagine what it will cost in eighteen years. The more money you can set aside for education today, the better prepared you'll be in future.

In Chapter 11, we'll talk more about planning for your child's education, as well as other ways you can help the children in your life.

WINDFALL OR INHERITANCE

It can happen. You get a larger-than-expected tax refund or a bonus for being a great employee. Your lucky number finally comes up in the lottery. Someone close to you dies and names you in their will. All of a sudden, you come into money.

A windfall or inheritance forces you to make a decision. Do you do something practical and boring with the money, like apply it to your line of credit? Or something fun and frivolous, like take an exotic vacation?

Our advice? If you've come into a modest amount of money, be practical. Use your $2,000, for example, to pay down your debt or add to your savings. Then make the exotic vacation a short-term goal in your budget. Save for it over time, and enjoy it.

It takes discipline to put unexpected money toward your debt or savings. A trip would be fun and exciting. Seeing your line of credit or mortgage drop by $2,000 isn't exactly thrilling. But a trip offers pleasure in the short term. Making your money work for you pays off in the long term. If you're not convinced, look back at Chapters 5 and 9, when we showed you how savings add up and how equity builds wealth.

What if it's a large amount of money? Maybe you've won a huge jackpot or inherited someone's estate. You're in a position to make some wonderful and life-altering choices. Do you pay down or pay off your mortgage? Invest the money so your retirement fund grows to where you'd like it to be? Buy an investment property and rent it out? Get a new car and take a trip to Europe? Help your kids with their education or a down payment on their first home?

These are all exciting choices. If you've received a large sum of money, you might be able to do something practical *and* something fun with it.

Whatever you do, don't rush into anything. Think hard about how best to use your newfound money. Talk things over with the trusted members of your team. The right choice can make all the difference to your future financial well-being—but so can the wrong choice.

A special word about inheritances. We urge you not to wait for an inheritance or plan around it. Make your own path with your own money and financial plan. If you do inherit, *then* change your plan.

The problem with assuming that you'll receive a bequest is that you may not. We've seen situations in which people were certain they'd receive most of the estate of a close family member only to be shocked when they didn't. In one case we know of, an individual had for years expected a sizable windfall and felt there was no need to save for retirement. When the expected amount didn't come through, the person was devastated and had to postpone retirement because quitting work was no longer an option.

Major life events affect us all. Babies enter the world screaming. Spouses drift apart. Someone wins the lottery. Children graduate. Businesses fail. People die.

Some changes are difficult and challenging, producing sorrow and stagnation. Others are invigorating and exciting, sparking growth in the garden of our lives. Some changes offer a bit of both: obstacles but also promises.

Tending your financial garden means watching it bloom and fade, year after year. It means staying vigilant and disciplined, keeping an eye on the far horizon, and doing what it takes to keep your plants alive.

The waiter came by. "Everything is fine, Madame Birch?" He eyed her untouched dinner.

"It's delicious, Michel. We're just taking a break."

Once the waiter disappeared, Rose spoke. "You said you didn't like Tripp at first, or trust him. What about now?"

Mrs. Birch placed a long-fingered hand over Rose's. "Oh, my dear. There's so much I can't tell you."

"Please." She needed to hear it.

"Do you know how I got into business?" Mrs. Birch leaned back. "When I was young, women didn't go into business. You might have a job, you could work as a secretary or assistant, or a teacher or nurse of course, but you didn't do deals. You didn't sit in the boardroom with the men and negotiate."

Rose only half-listened. What couldn't Mrs. Birch tell her about Tripp?

"My husband was much older than I. We married when I was twenty-five and he was fifty. Believe me, I've heard every interpretation of that relationship. Only one is true. We were very much in love. I was his secretary. He owned an import distribution company. I wasn't forty yet when he died. Heart attack at the office. Classic."

"I'm so sorry."

"It was a long time ago, my dear. Water under the bridge. He left me everything and the short story is I turned his everything into much, much more."

"Did you get married again?"

"No." She smiled sadly. "There was never anyone else for me. And now I've got other fish to fry. But that's not my point. I turned my husband's business into an empire. Really, it's not inaccurate to call it that. It helped that he had taught me a great deal, and I made smart decisions. But what I've relied on most over the years is my ability to read people. It's my biggest asset, and I've drawn on it again and again."

Mrs. Birch sipped more water. Rose waited. Was that it? Would she really reveal nothing more about Tripp?

"I know, for instance, that you were terribly hurt by your divorce." Rose's eyes flew open, and Mrs. Birch again reached for her hand. "Forgive me, but it's true, isn't it?" Rose hesitated, then nodded. "I also know it's hard for you to trust again. As for Tripp, there are many things about him I mustn't tell you. But I can tell you I was wrong about him from the beginning. Plain wrong. I am warming to him now, and this is for certain—I trust him completely."

11

The Children in Your Life

Laurel decided not to even approach her mother about babysitting today. She needed someone earlier than usual, and her mom stayed at the garden centre past closing these days. She called Jasmine straight away and offered her double pay to knock off work in time to get the boys at five.

"They'll be at their friend Rodney's, two blocks from school." She gave Jasmine the address. "You can cycle there, right?"

"Sure, sure," Jasmine shouted. The garden centre was hopping by the sound of things. "But how do I get them home? It's way too far to walk."

"Take them to the park down the street from Rodney's, the one with the play structures, and wait for me there. I'll meet you at five-thirty, six at the latest."

"Okay, but if you're going to be that early, why do you need me? Why not just leave them at Rodney's until you can pick them up?"

"Can't. That whole crew needs to take off as soon as you collect the boys. They've got tickets to something. Don't worry. The forecast is great, and Rodney's mom will give the boys a snack. They'll be fine running around for a while."

The arrangements never end, Laurel thought as she put her phone aside. You deal with one detail and two more pop up. She turned back to her computer. Twelve new emails! Her phone call had lasted, what, three minutes? How could there be so many? She drained the last of her stone-cold latte and willed herself to concentrate.

Five hours and she would be at the real estate office, listing her house for sale. Five hours and she would cast off the last tie to her old life, start drifting toward a new shore.

She knew selling was the right thing to do. She knew it. She just didn't feel it.

———※———

Children, like seedlings, are a symbol of optimism and faith in the future. Whether you're a mother or a grandmother, a guardian or a friend, you'll want the best for the children in your life.

TEACH YOUR CHILDREN WELL

Youngsters' physical and emotional security are vital concerns, but so is their financial security. Will they find the right career? Will they pay off their student loans? Can they afford housing? Will they earn enough to support themselves and, one day, a family of their own? Will they make sound financial choices while they're still young and as they grow?

Hold your kids close. But do them a favour: talk openly about their financial futures. Don't make money a taboo subject. Don't suggest that it's boring or off-limits for young people. Try not to instill any of the money fears we discussed in Chapter 2 or turn money into an emotional topic.

Instead, educate your kids about spending, saving, investing, and planning. Help them develop good money habits. Better yet, be a living, breathing role model. Show them what to emulate through your own sound financial behaviour. These are the responsibilities of a loving adult.

ఎ

There are lots of tangible things you can do to help the children in your life learn to be financially self-sufficient. You can give them gifts of money, with the proviso that they save or invest the cash. You can help them land their first job, whether it's babysitting for your friend or mowing the lawn for your neighbour. As they get older, you can co-sign their car loan, maybe contribute to the insurance.

If you have the means, helping the children you love can be a good way to launch them into their own lives. We support that idea—as long as it doesn't interfere with your own financial future. Self-sacrifice should only go so far; then you need to get a little selfish. If you're by nature a big giver, we encourage you to seek advice from your financial advisor to see what you can realistically do for your kids.

Keep in mind, too, that if you have four children, odds are that whatever you do for one, you'll want to do for all four.

In this chapter, we'll focus on two substantial steps you can take to help the children you care about: save for their education and help them with real estate.

SAVE FOR EDUCATION

Saving for your kids' education is one of the most valuable things you can do for them, because it has a multiplying effect. A better education equals better job opportunities, which puts your children farther along the path to becoming self-sufficient and managing their own financial future.

In an increasingly competitive world, education is a must. Years ago, an undergraduate degree was enough to open many career doors. Nowadays, it often takes an advanced degree for a job candidate to be taken seriously.

People can and do put themselves through university or technical college with a combination of student loans, bursaries, scholarships, their own savings, and income from jobs. But financial help from a relative or other caring adult can make a huge difference. It can reduce the burden of student loans that many grads carry for years, even decades, after their education is over. It can mean the student doesn't have to juggle a job and school, freeing up more time for studies.

Whether you're a parent or a grandparent, the best advice we can offer is to start saving early. The amounts don't have to be large. Time, perseverance, and the growth of invested money will go a long way toward building a nest egg for your loved ones' education.

One disciplined way to save for a child's education is to take advantage of a government-sponsored education savings plan. By setting up a plan that's earmarked for post-secondary education, and contributing to it regularly, you'll turn saving for education into a habit. You'll also ward off the temptation to spend the money on other, shorter-term needs.

An education savings plan is also a fund that others can add to—uncles, aunts, godparents, friends, anyone who wants to help your child get a leg up by furthering their education. A gift of a toy, clothing, or keepsake is always appreciated, but the gift of education provides benefits that last a lifetime.

HELP WITH REAL ESTATE

We believe that owning a home is better than renting and building up someone else's equity. Real estate is usually a smart long-term investment.

It makes sense that you'd want to see the adult children in your life enter the world of home ownership.

It can be tough for first-time buyers to put together a down payment and qualify for a mortgage. Here are four ways you can help your kids clear those first hurdles.

1. Give an outright gift of cash

If you have extra capital, a gift is the simplest thing to give, assuming no strings are attached. Remember, a gift is a gift. Once you've given it, don't expect repayment one day.

With this and any other financial help you give an adult child, it's important that you speak to your financial advisor and/or accountant about possible tax and other impacts.

2. Offer a loan with terms

You may decide to lend your child a sum of money, maybe at a lower interest rate than a lending institution would charge. Your loan can make the difference between your child's being able to scrape together a down payment or not.

This is a good option if you have other kids and want to treat them all equally. There's less risk of simmering resentment if the family gathers around the dinner table and hears talk about a loan that needs repayment rather than an out-and-out gift.

As good as it may feel to give a loan, we strongly encourage you to draw up a legal loan agreement. Say, for example, your child is married to someone you fear may not be around for the long term. You'll want the loan agreement to state that you can *call* the loan (ask for your money back) at any time.

3. Co-sign for a mortgage

You may opt to co-sign for your child's mortgage. By doing that, you're effectively telling the bank that if your child reneges on the debt, you'll step in and be responsible for repayment.

If you're thinking about co-signing a mortgage, first talk to your financial advisor and/or accountant. Do you want to hold legal title to the property? Are there any implications for your taxes or other real estate holdings?

4. Co-own a property

We've seen a number of clients invest in property with their children, though sometimes with little understanding of the wins or losses involved. When you co-own real estate, you need to think through all the eventualities, as well as each party's goals in the transaction—then get a tight legal document to reflect it all.

We believe co-ownership works only when there are advantages, financial or otherwise, for both parties. For example, we know of situations where a mom and dad convert their summer property into a four-season home and decide to live there year-round. However, they'd like a place of their own for those times when they come back to town to visit. A small suite or a dedicated room in their child's house, with the freedom to come and go as they like, may be just the answer.

Co-ownership may also make it possible for a family to have a holiday home. A vacation home may be beyond the means of one person, but splitting the cost two or three ways might make it affordable.

———— ∞ ————

A word of caution: Never starve a project. If you're going to help a child, you have to be able to give or lend enough to *increase* their chances of success. Giving just enough to start your kids off may doom the project or purchase because their cash flow over time isn't enough to keep things going.

The gift of a down payment, for example, can be immensely kind. But if high monthly payments mean your child has no life and is stressed out at the end of every month, was your gift really a good idea? We've seen some young people in tears because their cash flow is so tight. We've seen others build or buy grandiose homes far beyond their means, piling on loan after loan, with no hope of repayment.

You can offer your children support with the best of intentions, only to realize later that you've set up a different problem. Before lending your kids money for anything, make sure their plans are realistic and attainable. Otherwise, the results may be disastrous for you both.

And a word of inspiration: Teach your children well. One of the best things you can do for the kids in your life is to show them how to grow their own financial garden. Urge them to develop good habits early, to live within their means, to put money away for the future. Set a living example your children can look up to, not a bad example they'll have to live down.

Fifteen minutes before her appointment, Laurel was just exiting the office parking garage. The real estate office was fifteen minutes away without traffic, but the late afternoon rush had begun with a vengeance. She was cutting it fine.

She nosed onto the street, waved gratefully to the car that let her in. Heard the soccer ball thunk against the door as she made the turn. Stupid ball! She reached back to trap it. Why couldn't she remember to take it out, once and for all?

Twenty minutes later, she was four blocks from where she started. Officially late.

No, no, no! Her agent had to leave for a showing right after their appointment, and he'd urged her to arrive on time. Here she was, stuck, the exit to the highway half an hour away at this rate, never mind the ten-minute drive after that. She wanted to cry in frustration.

She had to take care of this. The SUV wasn't set up for hands-free calling—nice cost-saving measure there, Laurel, she thought. Pulling over wasn't an option; she'd lose her place in the sea of cars. It was against the law, but she felt she had no choice.

She fumbled in her purse, pulled out her phone. Furtively, trying not to telegraph what she was doing, she scrolled through her contacts—luckily she'd added the agent. Up ahead, the turnoff for Parkview. Yes! She could take that. Way faster than the street she was on now, and it led straight to the highway.

The agent sympathized but had to leave in half an hour. He offered to postpone. No way, she told him. She wanted this done.

She swung onto Parkview. Excellent! No traffic. She sped up, making up time. One more call, Al. This morning she'd agreed to meet him, finally, for coffee, a quick cup once she'd signed the listing. To celebrate, if you could call it that, putting her house on the market. A tiny step into another future.

No way could she meet him now. As it was, she'd be late picking up Jasmine and the twins.

She accelerated, glanced down at the phone in her hand, hit the Al icon.

There! The on-ramp to the highway. She was going to make it.

"Hello, Al?" The soccer ball thunked as she merged, swinging wide. "Al, are you there?"

As she floored it, she reached back with her phone hand to trap the stupid ball. Then thought better of it. Then the world, as she knew it, ended.

Part Four: Reaping

12

Planning for Retirement

It was the peaceful part of the day. The garden centre was locked tight, and Rose sat alone in the small front office, working through the books, getting a jump on her weekly report to Mrs. Birch. Numbers made so much more sense on paper. Thankfully, Mrs. Birch had trained her the old-fashioned way, with a ledger, calculator, and pen, not that horrible spread-sheet program Laurel was so fond of.

Software phobia aside, wouldn't Laurel applaud her mom now? It was official: She was the bookkeeper for the Blooming Tulip, with a raise to show for it. "Why me?" Rose had asked her boss. "Because you're sensible and I trust you," Mrs. Birch replied. "Besides, I have other fish to fry."

Weeks had flown by since Rose had properly visited her daughter. She would have to fix that. She'd largely stopped babysitting, hoping Jasmine would take over and wipe out her debts with the extra money. Rose knew Laurel could afford it; she billed so many hours at work nowadays. The strategy worked—Jasmine watched the kids two or three evenings a week now—but where did the money go? The girl still owed Rose a hundred dollars. "The Bank of Rose is closed," she'd said firmly when handing over the final twenty. Jasmine, true to form, wore a woeful face for five minutes before returning to her spritely self.

She had so much to tell Laurel. Her promotion. Her gleaming new bathroom, which Tripp finished last week and Laurel hadn't laid eyes on. And the whole Tripp business. The time had come to confide in her daughter: She might be in love.

Might be. Still Rose held back, clutching a small but unyielding plate of armour to her chest. It meant the world to her that Mrs. Birch trusted Tripp, but a veil still shrouded the man. He had past lives—as a renovator, a fine one, from what she could see, but he never spoke of it; and as a husband, to whom and for how long, Rose didn't know. He harboured secrets, and secrets made her wary.

Back to the books, Mom. Laurel's voice, clear, sensible, familiar, tugged her away from her dreams. The shrill peal of the office phone jolted her the rest of the way.

Retirement—some people long for it, some dread it, and some are undecided, not sure what this stage of life will bring.

If you follow the advice in this book, you'll spend much of your life planting and tending your financial garden, watching your investments blossom and your net worth grow, so that one day you can reap your rewards. If you're like many people, one of your sweetest rewards will be not having to set the alarm clock and go to work every day. Yet even if you've prepared well and long, hitting the runway of retirement can be one of the most emotionally fraught landings in life. Some people adapt wonderfully; others struggle.

When our clients are ready to retire, our main role is to discuss the financial and lifestyle implications of their decision. But we're also concerned about the practical and emotional changes they'll face. The excitement of retirement is often mixed with fear. It's important to get beyond that fear so that you can enjoy the many freedoms and rewards of this next chapter of your life.

Once you're ready to retire—or better yet, in the years leading up to retirement—you'll want to consult an advisor to review your financial plan and your tolerance for risk. When you retire and start to draw on your savings, you'll move from a savings plan to a maintenance plan, and that requires a different approach. You'll also want to review your goals. What will fill up your days when you're not working full-time?

We can't answer all your questions about retirement. But after years of helping people plan for and enjoy this time of life, we'd like to offer you our best advice in a few key areas.

HOW MUCH IS ENOUGH?

Have you saved enough for your retirement?

Enough is an interesting concept. "Have I saved enough?" is like asking "How long is a piece of string?" To a Buddhist monk, enough is knowing that an empty rice bowl will be regularly filled. Enough can be an appreciation of the beauty and simplicity of life. Or it can be a minimum of four stars (preferably five) on a hotel's website. Everyone is different in terms of Needs and Wants.

We'd like to think that if you've taken the advice in this book to heart, you'll have enough for your retirement. You'll have lived within your means, put money aside, and made that money work for you. You'll also have made the effort to dream about your future, set goals to get you there, and adjusted those goals over time. In other words, you'll have a good sense of what *enough* means to you.

All that's left, then, is to do some number crunching with your financial advisor. Review your financial plan and your budget. Your retirement income will come from several streams: government and employer pensions (if applicable), your own savings and retirement investment plans, and possibly rental real estate, the sale of an asset or a business, or other investments you've made over time. Make sure you understand each income stream and how secure it is. Then, and only then, will you know what you can spend each month, and whether it's enough.

Remember, too, that retiring doesn't have to mean giving up work entirely. More and more retirees are opting to work part-time or on contract, especially in the years right after leaving their full-time job. Working on your own terms can be a great way of topping up your income while still enjoying the freedom of the retired life. We'll talk more about this shortly.

WHEN TO RETIRE

Now we're going to get opinionated. We're generally opposed to youthful retirements. *What*, you ask? Isn't early retirement one of the rewards of following the advice in this book?

Yes and no. We want you to be in a position to retire, ideally by age 60, while you still have plenty of energy. An active mind, social interaction, and a sense of purpose all contribute to longevity. If you're sure you'll still have those things when you retire, and your finances are in good shape, go ahead and enjoy early retirement. If you dislike what you do, that's another good reason to go early. The stress of a job you hate may not be worth the extra money you'd build up by working longer.

But if you like what you do, don't retire young. We believe the healthiest retirement model—what we feel will be the model of the future—is to shift from working full-time to working part-time or project by project. Some of the most successful retirements we've seen involve working for a previous employer for a few months, then travelling for a few months, going back to work for a while, travelling again, and so on.

Retirees have valuable experience and smarts to offer the workplace. And today's retirees are healthier than previous generations were at the same age. That's why we think it will soon be common to see people working beyond the traditional retirement age of 65, whether they're starting a new business, consulting, or working part-time.

For you, a gradual transition from working a lot to working less will give you lots of flexibility, a sense of purpose, extra income, and continued contact with your colleagues and co-workers.

RETIREMENT FEARS

Retirement is one of life's milestones, but some are anxious about getting there. Our clients ask us a lot of worried questions. Who am I without my work? What's my purpose? What's my identity? Will I feel I've been sidelined after I stop working? How and where will I find a new network of friends? Will it make me crazy having my partner around all the time? Will I feel lonely without a partner? Will I face health or mobility problems? Am I on the slow march to death?

It's neither wise nor productive to focus on fears. Instead, focus on *possibilities*. The most successful retirees don't retire from something; they retire to something. And they don't try to fill their time; they try to enjoy it.

We encourage you to dream about your future. Let your dreams guide you to specific, attainable retirement goals. It's best if you do this dreaming well before you retire.

In your financial journal, write down all the things you want to accomplish in your life but have yet to do. Call it a bucket list if you will, but make it entirely your own. The items on your list may be as diverse as seeing the State Hermitage Museum in St. Petersburg, starting a blog, taking dance lessons, or going on a cruise.

Consider former hobbies, volunteering, and other pursuits you now have time for. Is that guitar still in the attic? Does the garden (or patio garden or community garden) capture your imagination? Look into adult classes, grab your camera, lace up your hiking boots, take a course on personal finance. Our friends have rebuilt cars, written books, painted stunning landscapes, kicked their cooking skills up a notch, gone skiing, learned a new language, volunteered in overseas orphanages, dental clinics and schools, and more.

Retirement is not about getting stuck in a holding pattern. It's a stage of life that offers no end of wonderful opportunities.

———

We believe in living with abundant grace and joy. We believe that you deserve happiness, but also that you're responsible for creating it. When you retire with a blooming financial garden around you, a new kind of happiness can begin.

As you prepare to retire, survey the garden you've created. Be proud of what you've made. Above all, *enjoy* it. Accept the rewards of all that planting, weeding, fertilizing, and nurturing. Your life will be richer for it.

———

This is not how it goes. You're supposed to age, gracefully if you're lucky, and watch your daughter, your only child, grow and thrive. Time passes, you get old, you die. Your daughter doesn't die. Your daughter stays alive.

Chills shot through Rose as she sat, hands in her lap, staring at the office wall. Some distant part of her knew she was in shock.

Get to the hospital, Mom. Laurel's no-nonsense voice, even now, prodded her.

Right, the hospital. Get there. Now.

Rose fumbled in her purse for her keys. *Don't drive, Mom. You're too upset. Get a cab.* That made sense. She took out her cell phone, turned it on.

If there's ever a time to turn on your cell phone, it's when your baby girl is in the trauma unit, fighting for her life. That's what cell phones were invented for.

Rose racked her brain for the name of a cab company, any name, any number. When the phone rang in her hand, she jumped.

"Rose, it's Jasmine. I'm worried. I've got the boys and Laurel was supposed to pick us up in the park half an hour ago. It's not like her to be late without calling, and I can't get her on her cell."

The girl's voice loosened something in Rose, and the tears fell like a tropical downpour, intense but blessedly short. Once she got herself under control, she told Jasmine everything. "Pile the boys into a cab and get to the hospital, okay? I'll meet you there."

"No, Rose! Don't hang up. I can't."

Breathe, Mom. Come on, breathe. Rose must still be in shock, because Jasmine wasn't making any sense. "Didn't you hear me? Laurel might die. Her boys, they have to be there."

Jasmine was sobbing, loud. "No, listen to me. I *can't.* I have no money. None!" Her words came fast and ragged. "I maxed out my last credit card at lunch today. I'm so sorry, Rosie. I can't do it!"

Breathe, Mom. Just breathe. "Okay, look. I'm going to call a cab. Tell me exactly where you are and I'll come get you. We'll go to the hospital together." The sobs continued. "It's okay, Jasmine. I'm coming."

Rose stood up. She remembered. There was a cab company number posted at the front cash.

You can handle this. You are her mother, she needs you to be strong.

Breathe, Laurel. Keep breathing.

13

Planning for End of Life

It was the longest night of Rose's life. Nothing compared; nothing even edged close. The divorce and all the despairing nights in its wake? Easy. Giving birth to Laurel, that nineteen-hour marathon of labour? Piece of cake.

They made an unusual quintet, she supposed. The distraught mother in dull, dirt-stained khakis, wooden one minute, sobbing into her hands the next. The young woman with cornrows and bell-bottoms, curled shrimplike across two seats, dreaming. The twin boys crash-landed somewhere between awake and asleep after their vending machine sugar high. The short, barrel-shaped British man, pacing and talking, first to his companions, then, as they retreated one by one into themselves, to the air.

Both medical people who had briefed them so far, the trauma nurse and later the surgeon, had uttered such maddeningly vague phrases that Rose longed to strike them, to *hurt* them. She's my daughter, she wanted to scream. Tell me exactly what is happening to her. From their reports, she retained only scraps: fractured pelvis, internal bleeding, blunt-force trauma, head injuries. The last was what terrified her. The rest sounded like things that would heal in time.

So surreal was this night that Rose had hardly blinked when, at around nine, Al appeared. Immediately he took her arm, pulled her into a corner.

"Rose, I heard it," he whispered. "The whole thing. It was so—" He shuddered. "Okay, that doesn't matter. It took me forever to track her down here."

"What do you mean, you heard it?"

"Ssh. You must whisper. Please. She had just called me, on her cell phone. Rose, we mustn't tell anyone. She's going to be held responsible, the police are saying as much. The angle of collision, and the witnesses . . . . But if they find out it was distracted driving, she could be charged."

Charged? What was he saying?

"The other driver got off easy. He was in a big van. He's just got a few stitches and some bruising. He's already back home with his feet up. But listen to me. Whatever happens to Laurel—" He broke off, closed his eyes tight. "Whatever happens, you need to get her phone and erase the log. Do you understand me? And if she wakes up—no, *when* she wakes up, you need to tell her. She's to say nothing about the phone. Not to anyone."

If you follow the advice we offer in this book, you'll put considerable work and care into preparing, planting, and tending your financial garden. Why?

Most of the reasons have to do with life. You want to live well and comfortably. You want to retire one day and have enough money to see you through the rest of your life. You want to protect and nurture yourself and those you share your life with.

What about death? When you're gone, what happens to this beautiful garden you've grown? Does it die with you? Or will you pass it along so that others can enjoy the fruits of your labour?

And how to do want to leave this world? Peacefully, with your affairs in order and your wishes clear, so that your loved ones know exactly what to do? Or stormily, leaving those closest to you to sort through the mess you've left behind?

Getting organized, setting goals, planning—these steps are just as important to successfully exiting life as they are to comfortably living it. If you're uneasy thinking about your own mortality, that's understandable. Many people are. In this chapter, we won't ask you to dwell on your death, but we will ask you to plan for it.

Failing to prepare for the end of your life can create all kinds of unanswered questions and unintended consequences. Worse, it can compound the pain and grief of the people you love. No good gardener leaves a tangle of weeds behind. Keep your garden blooming so that others can reap its rewards. It may even last for generations to come.

LIFE INSURANCE

Is anyone financially dependent on you? Do you perform tasks, such as caregiving, that others would have to be paid to do if you weren't there? Do you hope to leave money behind for people or causes you love?

If you answered yes to any of these questions, you need life insurance. A life insurance policy gives you the security of knowing that when you die, a specified sum of money will be paid out, tax-free, to your partner, child, or anyone else you name on the policy.

There are various types of life insurance to choose from. Some policies are permanent—they continue for your whole life, as long as you pay the premiums. Others are for a term—they apply for a specified length of time, or term, after which the policy ends. If you need coverage for only part of your life, when your expenses are high and your income is essential to others, term insurance may be right for you. If you're likely to renew the term later in life, a permanent policy may be a better option.

Your best bet is to explain your situation to a qualified insurance advisor. Advisors know the right questions to ask and can help you decide which type of policy suits your situation. They also have sophisticated computer programs at their disposal to help estimate how much coverage you'll need.

If you think you need life insurance, don't delay. The younger you are when you buy a policy, the lower your premiums will be. Insurers are reasonably confident that if you're young, you're in good health and not going to die soon. The irony is that you'll probably need more coverage when you're young. That's when you're most likely to have dependent children and large debts, like a mortgage.

POWER OF ATTORNEY

A power of attorney (POA) is a legal document that gives power, or authority, to one or more trusted individuals to act on your behalf when you're unable to make your own decisions. A POA takes effect when you decide to give that authority to someone else—if, for example, you go overseas and want to leave someone in charge of your affairs back home—or when you no longer have the capacity to make good decisions.

We believe that everyone, even young adults, should have a POA. A car accident, a bad fall, a brain aneurysm—it takes only an instant to go from being fine to being unable to make competent decisions. While it's not pleasant to contemplate, you do need to appoint an appropriate, trustworthy person while you're still of sound mind.

As the name suggests, there's a lot of power in a power of attorney. Your POA holder could, for example, direct money from your investment account to your chequing account, then write cheques to pay your expenses. You need a lot of faith in the person you appoint to act in your best interests. If you have a spouse or reliable adult children, they may be good choices for your POA. If you're single or have no kids, choosing someone becomes more difficult. If you have no fully trustworthy individuals in your life, we suggest you hire a law firm or trust company to fill this role.

Be sure to tell the person (or people) you choose where they can find your POA document. We suggest you file it in your personal estate binder, which we'll talk about near the end of this chapter.

A power of attorney ceases to apply as soon as you die. Once that happens, your will takes over. (We'll cover wills shortly.) Your will's *executor* becomes the voice of your wishes, just as the person you named as your *attorney* filled that role during your lifetime.

———

At seven in the morning, the unexpected smell of eggs and coffee drifting up from the kitchen one floor below, a new surgeon appeared, younger, with kind eyes. All of them were sleeping by then, except for Rose.

"You're Laurel's mother, right?" At the sound of her daughter's name, Rose trembled. The doctor touched her forearm. "It's okay. She's going to make it. She's a fighter, that girl of yours."

Now her tears fell freely. She swiped her face. "You have no idea."

Laurel ought to make a full recovery, the doctor said, given enough time and physio. It would be a day or two before anyone could see her. He suggested they all go home and check in later. Once he disappeared, Rose sat a moment, composing herself before waking the others.

"Rose." A large, warm hand cupped her shoulder.

She turned. "Tripp. How did you know?"

"What are you doing here?"

"Laurel, of course. Oh Tripp, she's going to be okay. Isn't that wonderful?"

He looked at her, puzzled. "Laurel? I'm here because of Mrs. Birch. Rose, I'm sorry to tell you. She's dead."

<hr />

LIVING WILL

Should a medical crisis seriously reduce your quality of life, you may have strong feelings about wanting, or not wanting, to remain on life support. A legally crafted living will, also known as an *advance health care directive*, *advance decision*, *medical power of attorney*, or *health care power of attorney*, will take difficult end-of-life decisions out of others' hands and put them in your own.

If you prepare a living will while you're still healthy and functioning, you're telling those closest to you that you've considered the matter carefully enough to have your instructions legally drawn up. Such a document can prevent or minimize family conflict during an already stressful time.

The requirements of a living will vary depending on where you live. Your lawyer or notary will know how to draft yours to meet the requirements of your jurisdiction.

Besides consulting a legal professional, it's a good idea to discuss your preferences and feelings with your family, so there are no surprises. We suggest you write a signed, dated letter in your own words to remind and reassure your loved ones of your wishes. Keep this letter and your legal document in your personal estate binder.

WILL

You've spent much, if not most, of your life nurturing and growing your financial garden. When you die, you want it divided up exactly as you wish. Making a will now, while you're alive, is the only way to make sure that happens. You can't do it when you are dead!

Your will is a written statement of directives to your appointed representative, or *executor*, to act precisely as you've indicated. If your will is well written, with little room for interpretation, there's an excellent chance your wishes will be honoured. If your will is not completely clear about who gets what, your estate could be tied up for a long time and your money could go to the wrong person.

Your will speaks for you when you are no longer here. It makes sure the people or groups you want taken care of after your death are indeed looked after. That makes your will one of your most important financial planning documents.

Use a qualified lawyer

We cannot stress enough how important it is to consult a lawyer who specializes in wills and estates. A general-practice lawyer may not be up to date on recent estate legislation. A specialist will be. A specialist will also ask probing questions about your wishes, priorities, and family structure before crafting a will that reflects everything you've said.

We've seen all kinds of inadvertent problems because people drafted their own wills and thought they'd done it right. You may intend to give each of your children an equal portion of your estate, but taxes on an inherited asset leave one child with less. You may leave money to someone who dies before you. Now who benefits from your estate? What's Plan B?

Speak to an estate lawyer about all the details that make your situation unique. A lawyer who specializes in estates is skilled and has likely seen every possible scenario. Do you have a family cottage to divide up? A family business? A child with special needs? If you have more than one heir, what's fair? Fair doesn't necessarily mean equal. Maybe one of your children housed you or your partner for years. Maybe one child, for whatever reason, needs more of a leg up than the others. The list of possibilities goes on and on. But we can tell you this—the sting of rejection from a badly crafted will can remain for years.

Is your life simple? Do you think you'll have few or no assets when you die? A will is still a good idea. It clearly states your final wishes so that no one has to guess. Above all, it makes the administrative side of your death easier for those you leave behind.

Choose a competent executor

Think carefully about who's in the best position to be named executor of your will. Don't base your choice on emotion but rather on suitability and competence.

You may think your sister will do a good job as executor of your estate, but you have to do your part and choose well. Your sister may be lovable and loyal, but is she organized? Reliable? Good with numbers? Diplomatic? Is she truly comfortable taking on the role of executor, or is she just agreeing to make you happy? If you have any concerns about your sister's abilities, or your estate is complex, it's probably wise to appoint a lawyer, trust company or other trusted person instead, or make them co-executor with your sister. It may cost more to hire a professional but it can be well worth the expense to have things done right.

Banks, insurance companies, and funeral homes offer free, step-by-step guides to the duties of an executor. We suggest you give one of these guides to anyone you're thinking about appointing so that they know what they are agreeing to.

Take the same care with any final wishes or instructions that go beyond your will. Say you want your best friend to organize an unforgettable wake. Or you want your niece to look after your miniature poodle. Communicate your wishes clearly. That doesn't mean dropping hints; it means putting your instructions in writing and storing them where they'll be found. A personal estate binder is the perfect storage place. We'll talk about that shortly.

Still numb, Rose lingered in the truck cab. She didn't want to leave this safe bubble for her ugly, empty apartment.

"Thank you for the ride. For everything." Even inside Tripp's fleece jacket, she shivered.

He touched something on the dashboard and warm air washed over her. "Come here." He gathered her in, the heat of him stronger and truer than the car's manufactured blast. "Everything's going to be fine. You'll see."

She had run through all her tears. Now there was only hollowness. The world around them lay quiet but for the rumble of the diesel engine.

Sitting there, the strength of Tripp's arm around her unfamiliar but inevitable, Rose remembered. "She kept saying she had other fish to fry. I thought she meant other companies to run. But she meant the cancer."

Tripp rested his chin on top of Rose's head. "I don't think anyone knew. Not even her daughter. When I called her, she didn't believe me at first."

"Daughter?"

"Mrs. Birch was a very private woman, wasn't she?"

Rose thought for a minute. "Does her daughter know about . . . the circumstances?"

"The pills? Yes. I left everything the way it was until she got there. Mrs. Birch thought her daughter would find her, I'm sure of it. She wasn't expecting me last night."

What exactly were you doing at Mrs. Birch's house, Rose wanted to ask, and at night? But this wasn't the time.

"There was a piece of paper on her night table," he said. "Not folded or anything. It just said 'Pancreatic, too hard, love to you all.' That was it."

Again Rose shivered.

Tripp tightened his arm around her and spoke into her hair. "Rosie." Despite herself, she smiled. Only Jasmine ever called her that. "Go on up, turn that rainhead shower on the hottest setting, and stay there as long as you can stand it. Then go to sleep. Okay?"

Saying yes to Lawrence Tripp was the easiest thing she'd done in a long time.

———◦∞◦———

PERSONAL ESTATE BINDER

Earlier in this book, we asked you to get organized—to get your files in order and keep a financial journal that contains your budget, long-term goals, dreams, and other notes. Besides making it easier to find things, keeping your documents together makes it easier to review and update your finances regularly.

Now we'd like to introduce you to your personal estate binder. A simple clip-in, clip-off, three-ring binder will do. In it, you will store all the documents that are part of organizing your estate.

Keeping everything in one place will greatly simplify the job of your executor, the person who holds your power of attorney, and anyone else who acts on your behalf at the end of your life. In fact, these people may add items to your binder, such as medical documents, copies of your death certificate, and funeral home paperwork.

Your personal estate binder will contain highly confidential material. Keep it in a secure place, such as a locked filing cabinet, a home safe bolted to the floor, or a safe deposit box. Make sure your executor, POA holder, and a trusted family member or friend know where your binder is and how to access it.

What to include

We've already mentioned many of the documents that should go into your personal estate binder. Here's a more detailed list, along with some important tips.

Personal contacts. At the front of your binder, list contact details for all the people and agencies that need to be notified if something happens to you. This list will get you started:

- Next of kin, other family
- Close friends
- Close neighbours

- Employer, close co-workers
- Doctor, dentist, other health professionals
- Agencies, charities, churches, clubs, and other organizations you're closely associated with

Estate, legal, and banking contacts. Include current contact information for everyone with an administrative role in the end of your life:

- Power of attorney holder
- Executor
- Lawyer or notary
- Insurance agent
- Tax accountant
- Banker
- Financial advisor

List all your bank and investment accounts and any pension details. If you're a renter, include your landlord's contact details, your rental agreement, and your tenant insurance. If you're a homeowner, include details of your property taxes, home insurance, and homeowners' association (if applicable). Include a copy of your life insurance policy.

Confidential material. Put your most confidential material in a sealed, signed envelope clipped to the inside of your binder. Mark the envelope to be opened by your executor only (or POA holder if appropriate). Confidential material might include the key to your safe deposit box and passwords for your computer, email, banking, blogs, and other online accounts.

Power of Attorney. As we said earlier, make sure this document is legally crafted and up to date. Your POA holder may need to access documents in your binder, so tell that person where to find it.

Living will. A copy of the official legal document belongs in your binder. So does your personal letter that outlines your final wishes on critical health matters. Remember to sign and date your personal letter.

Will. Include a photocopy of your up-to-date will. It's best to keep the original signed document on file with your lawyer or notary, in a safe deposit box, in a locked filing cabinet, or in a home safe bolted to the floor. In your binder, note where the original will is so that your executor can find it.

Executor information. If you've picked up a free executor's guide from a bank, insurance company, or funeral home, include it too. Write down, sign, and date any special instructions for your executor beyond what's in your will. For instance, even though your power of attorney and living will end at your death, ask your executor to keep both on file in case of legal or family disputes.

Information about dependants. If you have children or others who depend on you, leave instructions for how they should be taken care of. We've known of couples who couldn't decide who should look after their children in the event of an untimely death. Instead of designating someone they could agree on, they left *no instructions at all*—and no will. As hard as it is to make such decisions now, it will be far harder for someone else to decide if you're not here.

Funeral arrangements. Do you want to be cremated or buried? Do you want a large memorial service that anyone can attend, or an intimate gathering of friends and relatives, or no service at all? Have you already paid for your funeral or your burial plot? Have you written your own obituary, or is there someone you'd like to choose for the task? Put all these details in your binder.

Other end-of-life instructions. Do you have family heirlooms, wedding china, or other personal belongings to distribute outside your will ? Include an itemized list. Do you have pets? Include the details of who will take care of them. Do you have secret recipes or a sheaf of poems to pass along? Put the details in your binder.

Keep it current

Consider your binder a work in progress. You'll need to update it from time to time as your circumstances and people's contact details change.

We recommend that you review your formal estate documents—your power of attorney, living will, and will—every three years. Remember, too, to periodically review any accounts or policies that name a beneficiary. Many people forget to change beneficiary information on things like their employer-sponsored life insurance and pension plans when their lives and relationships change.

To help keep your binder current, make a to-do list on the first page. List any pending updates and reminders to yourself, particularly for things you plan to add or change when the time comes. Keeping all your reminders in one place will make your updates much easier, whether they're formal revisions (to your power of attorney or will) or informal (to your instructions about dependants or your funeral).

Whenever you update your binder, remove and destroy any pages that no longer apply. Be sure to sign and date any new and revised documents.

Just as everyone's end-of-life wishes are unique, so is each personal estate binder. Ask yourself what information *you'd* like to see if you were your own executor.

LEGACIES AND FOUNDATIONS

We've talked a lot about the end-of-life arrangements you should make for family and others close to you. Those are some of the most important decisions you can make. But now, put family considerations aside for a moment and consider the broader scope of your life. Outside your inner circle, what do you value? Community? Politics? International aid? Education? The sciences?

Think about what these values have meant to you, and what you, through your ongoing support, have meant to them. What will happen when you're no longer around to volunteer or write that monthly or yearly cheque?

You don't have to be extravagantly wealth to leave a legacy. We've been astounded at the people of seemingly modest means who have come into our offices prepared to make a large charitable gift to an organization they admire. Surprises abound everywhere. You, too, have the opportunity to create some lovely surprises.

Your legacy is about your priorities. Do you want your name on the side of an arena? Or on the church pew where you sat in life? Do you see yourself sponsoring an arts grant or donating to your local hospital? Think about the kind of legacy you'd like to leave, and for whom.

A one-time donation is fairly easy to arrange. It takes a bit more planning to set up a legacy in perpetuity—say, a scholarship or bursary to a promising first-year student at your alma mater. The members of your planning team can arrange a bequest like this through a foundation or a donor-advised fund (a mini-foundation without all the paperwork).

What if you don't have enough money to establish a foundation of your own? Many cities have community foundations, which put small and large sums of money to benevolent use without you or your heirs having to administer the fund. Community and philanthropic foundations exist throughout the world, and they oversee billions of dollars in local assets. They fund scholarships, the arts, neighbourhood help for needy kids, and many other initiatives that leave a lasting legacy—and that could be part of *your* legacy.

Tripp looked fidgety, one leg jumping as he leafed nonstop through magazines. No wonder, Rose thought, taking in his sports jacket and the button-down collar he kept fiddling with.

Of course, a lawyer's office rarely passed for an oasis of relaxation. Rose too felt the fingers of anxiety tighten around her shoulders. They had been summoned here, but neither knew why.

Tripp looked up and smiled. Rose's heart did its usual somersault, but with the sensation came a deeper feeling. Gratitude, maybe, that he was there with her. "How's everything at work?" she asked.

"Fine. We miss you."

"I'm coming back on Monday." It was time. With Laurel's condition stabilized and the twins back at school, she needed her routine back. She missed the garden centre, the other staff, the customers. And the work. She wanted—needed—to make something grow. "Why are we here, anyhow?"

Tripp shrugged. "Beats me. Her whole family's in there." He nodded at the closed boardroom door. "Must be something about the business."

The penny dropped, and Tripp met her startled gaze with one of his own. "You don't think . . .", she began. But she knew. The Blooming Tulip was a tiny piece of a huge corporate puzzle. There could be only one reason they were there. "Oh, no," she said. "All those jobs. All the work we did to bring the place back. Tripp, what are we going to do?"

14

Living a Life in Bloom

For the first time since landing in the hospital, Laurel could honestly say she felt better. She hurt more—she hurt everywhere—but at least she'd come out of the painkiller fog. The doctor balked at cutting her dosage, but she wore him down, the benefit of being a talker. "First I need my mind back," she told him. "Then I can work on my body."

Cards and bright bouquets dotted the tiny room. In the place of honour, atop a table near the foot of her bed, stood a lavish arrangement from the Blooming Tulip. "I put in freesia," said Jasmine, "for the smell. At least your nose isn't hurt."

Laurel's mother almost matched the room for cheer, today wearing her favourite lilac blouse and a necklace of purple and silver beads. She showed up twice a day, morning and evening, like clockwork. Laurel had never loved her more.

"So, any decisions?" Laurel asked.

"We're keeping it, running it as partners." Rose smiled shyly. "Bet you never saw your mom as a businesswoman."

The news still astounded Laurel. The elegant Mrs. Birch had left the Blooming Tulip to her mom and Tripp, half and half, under one condition:

They could each do what they wanted with their half, keep it or sell it, but the business had to continue.

"It means I can help you out honey, with the physio costs, legal fees, anything." Laurel began to protest, but her mother cut her off. "Not a loan, a gift. You can count on your father too. You should have gone to him long ago, before things got so bad. He's crushed that you didn't ask for help."

Laurel couldn't believe her ears. "You talked to *Dad*?"

"He's here. He flew in yesterday. He'll come by this afternoon." Rose reached over and hooked a piece of hair around Laurel's ear. "You're our daughter, honey. We want to help you. But you have to let us."

"I know. I just . . . I really thought I could handle it."

Her mother smiled and shook her head. "Your whole life you've been so strong. Ever since you were little. When Matthew died . . . well, some people would never get over a thing like that. But you did. You picked yourself up and you got on with life, and you'll do it again." She took Laurel's hand. "It's okay to need other people, honey. We all do. It doesn't make you less strong. It takes strength to ask for help. You hear me? Strength. Not weakness."

―⁂―

Part Four of this book is about reaping. That word, to us, means a lot of things. It means harvesting the financial garden you've sown throughout your life. It means protecting your harvest so that it lasts you through retirement to the end of your life. It means distributing what's left among your loved ones after you're gone.

But financial rewards are only part of it. We believe you should reap *all* the rewards of a life well lived through hard work, discipline, wisdom, and patience.

REAP YOUR REWARDS

Money, as we've said before, has no value on its own. It's only worth what you exchange it for. In the same way, your worth, and the worth of your life, can't be summed up by a number on a piece of paper. Your worth comes from what that number brings you.

During our working life, we often train our sights on the rewards of retirement. But doing that can obscure an important fact: Life is not some giant end game. Life's intrinsic gift is life itself, in all its messy, wonderful abundance. Waiting to live your "real life" in some distant future is hardly living. Likewise, saving without spending is joyless. Sure, retirement is a big part of reaping your rewards. But so is going on that great holiday, learning a new skill, or donating to your local homeless shelter.

Our advice: Save well, but spend well too. Understand what money is for. Don't hoard it for its own sake. Use it to nurture yourself, your loved ones, and your community throughout your life.

We wrote this book to share our advice on how to plan, save, and invest well. We'd like to close with some thoughts about how to protect your independence, how to live well, and how to turn financial security into a life that's rich in every respect—a life in bloom.

—∞—

For days Laurel thought about her mother's words. *It takes strength to ask for help.*

If that was true, then she'd be a bodybuilder by the time she got out of here, because everyone was helping her. In no time she'd acquired a whole team. Her parents. The medical staff. Her boss, who was holding her job once again. Jasmine, who had moved in to watch the twins when she wasn't at work or college, where she was studying horticulture. And Al, who picked up the slack. Every day he picked up the boys at school and brought them to see her. He took them home, fed them, and played games (too many, from what Laurel heard) until Jasmine arrived. He brought Laurel things she needed, and things she didn't know she needed.

It was the oddest thing, the way Al had slipped into her life. Since that one chance meeting at the garden centre, she had heard his voice nearly every day, first in his persistent phone messages, now in person. He even set his phone to vibrate while he was teaching in case she needed him.

He had a hard time, at first, accepting Laurel's refusal to hide her distracted driving. She had caused the accident, pure and simple. The blame was hers alone. So far no one was threatening legal action and the other driver seemed content to let the insurance companies work out the details, but that could change. If it did, she would deny nothing. After Matthew's accident, after the long struggle to see his killer convicted, what kind of person would she be, what kind of mother, if she didn't own up to her mistake?

She had explained all this to Al. She had told him so much more from this hospital bed, and he had done the same sitting beside her. His company felt easy and bubbly, like a warm bath, and she teetered on the edge of sinking in, just letting go. He would be there, she knew, to keep her afloat.

Laurel had received so much help. But that wasn't, she realized, what her mother said. It takes strength to ask for help, was what she said. It takes strength to *ask*.

PROTECT YOUR FINANCIAL INDEPENDENCE

We believe that happiness stems from appreciating what you have now. We urge you to safeguard what you have by protecting your financial independence.

If you're a single adult and you run your own life, chances are you're already financially independent. If you're in a relationship or about to enter one, it's important to look at your financial arrangements. Do they protect you and the financial garden you're growing? Or do they leave you wide open?

We've watched great love stories unravel over money and have had to hold our tongues as people make what we feel are colossal relationship and financial errors. We'd like to pass along what we've learned from these experiences.

Shared lives, shared finances

We've seen couples handle their finances in myriad ways, good and bad.

We've seen spreadsheets used as a team-building exercise to answer the question: *What's our joint financial plan?* We've seen spreadsheets used as an instrument of cruelty, sabotage, and control.

We've seen couples in their eighties, married for six decades, still keeping separate bank accounts and detailed ledgers of who spent what. We've seen full mergers in which the joint chequing account always has just enough money to prevent a bounced cheque.

We've seen couples split their expenses 50-50. At first glance that seems fair, but as we said in Chapter 13, fair doesn't necessarily mean equal. The problem comes when the two incomes aren't even close to being equal. Under a 50-50 arrangement, one partner may resent having to pay for half a lifestyle he or she might not otherwise choose. One partner may resent having to scale back because the other lacks the funds for a world cruise or other extravagance.

However you and your partner decide to arrange your finances, we urge you to stay *actively involved and aware.*

If you're already in a long-term relationship and tend to leave financial matters to your partner, changing may be hard. You don't have to do it all at once. It's fine to build your involvement bit by bit.

You owe it to yourself to learn a little about a lot of things so you can keep the wheels of your life turning. We have clients who come to our office only because their spouse asked them to. If they're lucky, they only need to sit in on every second meeting. Sometimes they gaze out the window or at a piece of art, but we appreciate that they're *there.* The relationship they are building with us will benefit them if they suddenly find themselves alone.

If you're in a new relationship, protecting your financial independence may mean entering into a domestic partnership agreement, as we discussed in Chapter 10. Make sure your relationship feels fully comfortable, and you and your partner have built a firm foundation of trust, before divulging your wealth and sharing your assets.

A wise friend of ours told her daughter, "Start the way you intend to finish." The patterns you set at the beginning of a relationship are the ones that will stick. Lay out your ground rules, standards, expectations, and participation. The time you spend drawing those lines—or redrawing established lines, if you're already in a relationship—is immensely important.

The best relationships are those in which two people see themselves as partners in the same small rowboat, pulling together. They have a clear vision of their present and their future, they love each other enough to fall into generosity, and they don't keep score. Neither resents the other's spending, and neither takes all the praise for the positive choices they've made in life.

Our beliefs about financial independence

We believe both partners should be aware of their household finances. It may fall to one to handle the regular financial tasks, such as paying bills, reviewing investments, filing statements, and updating the financial plan, but the other needs some involvement. Consider the widows and widowers who lose their handyman, cook, mechanic, social director, *and* bookkeeper when they lose their spouse.

We believe in honesty and full disclosure. We've seen people hide purchases and credit card bills for months, and when the day of reckoning comes, it's never pretty. It's not right to spend irrationally and create future risk. We've seen couples forced into bankruptcy because of the profligacy of one mate. We knew a woman in her early seventies whose husband died unexpectedly. Unaware of their true financial picture, she soon went from grief to anger. Gone was the country club lifestyle and the other perks she'd known. The last we heard, she was a cashier at a car wash. Why should one person's life have to change dramatically because of another's irresponsibility and dishonest communication?

We believe you should have a pot of money to call your own. You don't have to be accountable to anyone for this pot—we'll respectfully assume that you and your partner are adults and deserve to be treated as such. If you buy your partner a gift, there's no need for the money to come from a joint account or for your partner to know the cost. If you value a monthly facial or a round of golf or fancy footwear, and your partner doesn't, having your own money is especially important. It means you can make spending decisions that satisfy you without affecting your family's financial plan and overall security.

We'll say it again: Protect your financial independence. Protecting yourself means you'll never be a victim. You'll never be surprised by your financial status. You'll have your own money. You'll have autonomy. And who knows? You may even have a better relationship.

⚬❀❀❀⚬

The parking lot stretched out, empty, the Blooming Tulip sat silent. Mrs. Birch's memorial was this afternoon, but the staff voted to close the store all day. Rose and Tripp announced that everyone would be paid half a day's wages; privately they settled on a full day if the books looked good.

Tripp punched in the alarm code and Rose trailed him to the office, admiring the cut of his sport coat, the same one he'd worn to the lawyer's. "The monkey suit," he called it, tugging at his shirt collar, when he picked her up.

When she bent over to open the ledger, a lock of hair came loose. Tripp's fingers wound themselves in it, gently, tentatively. "Rose."

She looked up. She was getting better at meeting that intense blue gaze. A good thing too, if they were going to work as partners.

His hand moved from her hair to her cheek. "It's exactly the right name for you. Beautiful as a rose."

Her cheeks flamed. Red like a rose too, she thought wildly.

He drew one thumb along her cheek. "Does this bother you?"

"You know it doesn't."

He laughed gently. "You're right. We're too old to play games, aren't we? I'm tired of pretending. The first time I walked into this place, do you remember? It was a staff meeting, so everybody must've been here, but the only face I saw was yours. That's still how it is for me. That's how it's always going to be."

Rose swallowed. He could be describing her feelings, because she felt exactly the same way. She longed to say that. She felt like she knew Tripp, had known him all her life, yet so much of his life hid in shadows. He was right, they were too old to play games. She wouldn't play.

CHOOSE GROWING

How would you like to be remembered when you're gone? What statement do you hope others will make about you? And what about now—if you could sum up your life in a single sentence, what would it be? Are the two statements consistent, or is there a gap between them? Is the person you are now the person you aspire to be?

No life is perfect. There is always room for growth. You have within you the capacity to grow in many ways. To return to our garden analogy, everyone is growing, wilting, or dying. We urge you to *choose growing*.

Think of growing as your personal legacy. Just as a legacy can be a gift of money or property, it can also be the memories you leave behind, the example you set, the love you give and receive, and the generosity you show in life and in death.

Many factors contribute to a rich and successful life, one that grows through every stage and blooms for all to see. Here are the attitudes we think matter the most.

Be open to change

Being unable to accept and embrace change will hold you back and age you faster than anything we know. You may not want to shift careers, but if a new job opens up a better future, surely it's worth the leap. You may be afraid to remarry, but you can at least acknowledge your fears and consider it. You may feel destined to live in your house forever, but a place with a smaller garden might free up time for things you enjoy more. We've seen clients make life changes like these with great success.

Do the proverbial mirror check: look yourself in the eye and ask what is and isn't working for you. Then ask what you really need and want. That's hard. We're often better at seeing what others need than what we need ourselves. Remember, change can be good. Don't let fear, history, or other people hold you back. Consult? Sure. Think carefully? Absolutely. But don't let yourself become ossified.

Budget to have money in the bank

You can have anything you want—you just can't have everything. If your parents were wise, you learned that lesson as a child. If *you* were wise, you learned it or relearned it as an adult. We hope you'll pass the message on to the children in your life.

Create a plan for what you can spend each year and make your choices from that. There are always abundant choices. We have friends whose bucket list included travel who wrote down all the places they wanted to see. They focused on their finances so they'd have the budget to follow their dreams. Time and energy forced them to prioritize their list. They won't get to Antarctica this year, but they're on their way to Zanzibar.

Budget for social outings

You may grimace at the price of a "cuppa joe," especially when the joe is an extra-large caramel mocha extra-whip latte, but the emergence of today's coffee culture is an important social shift. Financial advisors often say that if you set aside the cost of your daily designer coffee, you'll save $1,000 a year. There are times when that's wise counsel—instead of buying the coffee, and the sandwich or pastry that goes with it, take a walk with a friend and bank your cash. But on a cold day when the rain or snow won't stop, a cup of coffee, a bowl of soup, or a matinee and popcorn with a friend does more than warm the insides.

Healthy lives involve social contact, and that means face time, not just screen time. Outings with friends and family will enrich you throughout your life. They're especially important once you retire and aren't seeing co-workers every day. Plan and budget for get-togethers with the people whose company you enjoy.

Be the person others want to be with

Every one of us has problems, from job frustrations to aches and pains to marital woes and worse. You have every right to talk about your troubles with the people you trust. But please, whatever happens in your life, don't become that person who's always negative, bitter, and no fun to be around. That person often ends up alienating friends and family, and even acquaintances, all because of negativity.

Financial negativity is part of the picture. Constantly complaining about inflation, the cost of living, and the size of your paycheque or pension won't get you anywhere. If you're truly concerned about money, discuss your worries with a good friend, or better yet your financial advisor, and make a plan for dealing with them. You'll feel better, and those around you won't have to suffer through your griping.

We encourage you to nurture your inner optimist. When things are bad, work through the problems, learn from them, and move on. When things are good, spread your happiness. Laugh more; complain less. Make your life bigger, not smaller. That's what growing is all about.

Savour the joy of anticipation

Though you should never wish your life away, you need something to look forward to. It may be planning next year's vacation, awaiting your first grandchild, saving for a new car, getting a jump on the next garage sale, or anticipating retirement.

Whatever your goal, don't let impatience get the best of you. Savour the time it takes to get there. That "I can hardly wait" feeling adds a sprinkle of excitement and joy to life.

Volunteer your time

Almost everyone who reaches the magic age of 100 says that a secret to their longevity is a sense of purpose, engagement with others, and involvement in their community. Even if you don't want to live to 100, no matter how long you're around, volunteering is a wonderful and generous way to enrich your life.

Volunteering is most rewarding when both sides benefit, so choose an activity that's meaningful to you as well as valuable to others. Join a horticultural society, deliver meals to the homebound, join a board of directors, or take on a duty in your mosque, temple, or church. Whatever it is, think about adding at least one weekly and monthly commitment to your life.

Once they retire, some people build a career out of volunteering. Even if you don't go that far, you may find the transition to retirement easier if you have enjoyable, non-paying jobs lined up to keep you busy.

Safeguard your health

As one of our friends puts it, we're all TABs—Temporarily Able-Bodied. Enjoy good health while you have it, and as you age, do whatever you can to keep your body, mind, and soul in the best condition possible. Sure, financial health matters, but what good does it do if you're too sick or weak to enjoy it?

Make your health a priority throughout your life. We're all for investing in stocks, but money you spend on nutritious food and physical activities is one of the best investments you can make. If health problems plague you, don't ignore them. Seek the treatments you need and build the cost into your financial plan. If you need a physiotherapist to recover from an injury or stay mobile, put that in your budget. If you have to, cut elsewhere to make room for spending on health.

We hope that, besides being in great financial shape, you'll be FAB— Fully Able-Bodied (and fabulous)—as long as you can.

"I'll tell you everything, Rose. Anything you want to know." They were seated now, side by side, in the office, Tripp's hands pressed between his legs. "I'm sick of secrets. They were more Mrs. Birch's idea than mine anyhow."

"Let's start with her. Did you have a . . . thing with her? Or were you related or something?"

He laughed sharply. "We had a relationship all right, but not the kind you're thinking of. Where do I even start?" He pushed a hand through his hair. "Okay. I have a sister. A twin, actually. Cathy. That name mean anything to you?"

"Should it?"

"No, I guess not. Different last names and all. Cathy Ramsey."

Rose drew back. "Cathy *Ramsey*? She hired me here. Though I never saw her again after the interview."

"No. She left town. I spent a couple of months trying to track her down, but she's gone, as in disappeared without a trace. She left a real mess behind, a huge mess. Not just the Blooming Tulip—well, you remember the state it was in—but she had another business, this vitamin and supplement distribution company, with an investor behind it. An investor I introduced her to."

The connection fell into place. "Mrs. Birch?"

"Right. I didn't know her and I'd never worked with her before, but this guy from my company had."

"Your company?"

He smiled. "Bathroom renovation, what else? I started it when I was twenty, just a stupid kid. Stupid enough to have no clue what I was getting myself into. Stupid enough to get married too, when I wasn't ready for it. The timing couldn't have been worse. I worked all day every day, and most of the evening. I never saw her but I figured she'd stick around anyway. She fixed that pretty quick. Left me flat." He shook his head. "Only thing it did was throw me more into work, and I ended up with a great big high-end business."

"No wonder my bathroom's so perfect." Relief coursed through Rose. She had told herself much darker stories about Tripp's marriage, tales of anger, disloyalty, and cruelty. This, she could handle.

"Anyhow, as for Cathy, when she took off she hadn't paid one cent back to Mrs. Birch, and the vitamin business, if you want to call it that, was worthless. I felt responsible. It was me who set Mrs. Birch up with Cathy. So I cut a deal. Mrs. Birch could take the Blooming Tulip as payment for what Cathy owed her. It was a gamble, but for Mrs. Birch it was better than zero. I sweetened the pot by throwing myself in, for free. Seemed like a new landscape design service couldn't hurt."

"For free?" What Tripp said hung together, but she was struggling to absorb it all.

"Why not? I sold my business five years ago and was doing some landscape design anyway. Just a retirement project, something to keep busy." He reached forward and took her hand. "Rose, it was my fault. That's the thing. Mrs. Birch is . . . was a smart investor. She'd never have pumped money into my sister's crappy business if I hadn't vouched for it."

"No wonder she was so awful to you at the beginning."

"I know. She must have hated me. But I had to do whatever I could." He leaned in closer. "I was responsible. That sits heavy with me, Rosie. You need to know that if we're going to be partners." He kissed her hand. "Of any kind."

Rose felt the familiar warmth of a blush steal over her. But so what? This was life, after all: these feelings, these stories, this responsibility to others, this heat blooming in her cheeks.

―――∞∞∞―――

Financial advisors view much of life through a lens of financial consequences. But we also understand that holding bank accounts, investments, and real estate brings comfort on many levels, not just physical. We know that having a financial backstop can give you the security and confidence you need to explore other aspects of your life.

We hope this book has taught you many valuable lessons about how to grow a blooming financial garden. We also hope it's taught you some indirect lessons about life. After all, what's the point of a rich and varied portfolio if not to enrich and deepen your life?

We can't make your decisions for you, but we hope you'll live a life of gratitude and generosity. We hope you'll be as happy as you can possibly be. That means pausing to appreciate what you have today, not just what you may have in the future.

Be prudent, of course, but also dream. Live the life you truly want to live. Hug your children. Give to others without expectation of recognition or thanks. Find your happiness, and hold it close.

Acknowledgments

We would like to thank the following people for their time, energy, support, insight and sharp eyes in reviewing our work: Barbara, Susan, Alexia, Lynne, Cathy and to all who provided input along the way.

We would like to give special thanks to Frances Peck of Westcoast Editorial Services for all of her editorial work and creativity.

Justin Dyer remembers watching the stock market as a child. Both of his parents worked in finance, and their passion was passed on to their son. Justin has been working in the investment industry since 1994 and is a Fellow of the Canadian Securities Institute. He lives in North Vancouver, Canada, and is an accomplished Toastmaster.

Nancy Farran is a Fellow of the Canadian Securities Institute and has been helping people manage their finances and investments for over thirty years. An investor herself since an early age, she is passionate about helping others learn to manage their own money well. She enjoys volunteering in the community and spending time with family. She lives in West Vancouver, Canada.

Made in the USA
San Bernardino, CA
28 November 2018